# IF I MUST DIE

# IF I MUST DIE

## Poetry and Prose

# REFAAT ALAREER

Compiled by Yousef M. Aljamal

With a foreword by susan abulhawa

**O/R**

OR Books

New York • London

Published by OR Books, New York and London

Visit our website at www.orbooks.com

All rights information: rights@orbooks.com

First printing 2024

Library of Congress Cataloging-in-Publication Data: A catalog record for this book is available from the Library of Congress.

British Library Cataloging in Publication Data: A catalog record for this book is available from the British Library.

Cover design and typesetting by Antara Ghosh

Printed by BookMobile, USA, and CPI, UK.

hardback ISBN 978-1-68219-621-2 • ebook ISBN 978-1-68219-622-9

Refaat Alareer

(September 23, 1979–December 6, 2023)

# Contents

# Foreword

On December 7, 2013, a Ph.D. student in Malaysia reached out to me by email because he was writing a research paper on a section of *Mornings in Jenin*. He told me that he had taught my novel at the Islamic University of Gaza, and he hoped to get my thoughts on his thesis. His name was Refaat Alareer. We corresponded on the topic and kept in touch. We became friends and comrades, and I came to love, respect, and value him.

Exactly ten years later, on the morning of December 7, 2023, I awoke to news that Israel had killed Refaat. They targeted the home where he had taken refuge the previous day, and it took a day for news to trickle out of Gaza's blackout. I sat in front of my screen, red-eyed and in shock, searching for remnants of Refaat in my own life—signed books, notes, photos, messages, and emails. I quickly discovered that the email in 2013 was not my first encounter with Refaat. I found an earlier message, from 2011, in which I told a friend that I had cried over a beautiful tribute to Vittorio Arrigoni, the Italian solidarity activist who was killed in Gaza. The tribute was written by a Refaat Alareer. I had not made the connection until I went searching for him after Israel killed him.

Much of the correspondence between Refaat and me was conducted over Twitter (now rebranded as X). But my account was permanently suspended in early 2023 after Zionists launched a campaign to have me canceled, and all of those messages were stolen from me. Although that account had contained an audit of my thoughts and activism for at least a decade, I never mourned its loss until I needed to re-read my exchanges with Refaat.

Shortly after Israel launched its genocidal assault on Gaza, Refaat urged me to create a new Twitter account. Always trying to make our case to the world, he said, "we need your insight there," and he suggested a handle for the account. I immediately did as he counseled and sent the link to him. His response: "Got your first 4 follows [wink emoji]."

He was smart to have multiple accounts, prepared with backups in case of social media assaults. His mind was unbreakable and beautiful and fine. Online trolls and cancellation campaigns were no match for him. But he had no defenses against bombs. The most dangerous thing he had was "an expo marker," as he told Ali Abunimah in his last interview with the Electronic Intifada. He said he would throw it at soldiers when they broke into his home. But he would not even get the satisfaction of that imagined small moment of self-defense. Israelis, cowards as they are, targeted him from the sky.

Three days before Israel murdered Refaat, he sent me a video of what remained of his home and the lifetime of memories it held. The video records three and a half minutes of him walking through unimaginable destruction in Tel al-Hawa, narrating the life that used to be, pointing to pieces of things once whole, clean, functional. A sofa, where he had perhaps lounged lazily countless times, maybe with a book, his children climbing on him; a broken window frame that brought breeze and sunshine and kept in the warmth of the family he loved and lived for; a piece of cloth, like the one in the poem he wrote for his daughter Shymaa, "If I Must Die."

The heartbreak he must have felt is difficult to fathom. Refaat was no stranger to injustice and profound loss. Israel murdered his brother and at least thirty members of his wife's family in 2014, one of many aerial pogroms committed against Palestine, Gaza in particular. But "this [time] is different," he told me in a text on October 14. He wrote, "it's going to be even worse. We are bracing for that. We have no way to defend ourselves."

I believe some part of him knew what was to come. Still, he was planning for things "after the genocide stops." In particular, we talked about the Gaza Zoo. It pained him that many of the animals died because they had gone without water or food for weeks. Two days later, on October 16, I messaged to check on him after Israel began bombing Shujaiya. Of the people murdered that day, he said, "it's my relatives. But I don't know who. Calls can't reach."

In the video, Refaat continues walking, narrating what we can all see but cannot truly comprehend. Hearing his voice in that recording now is strangely soothing, as if he's not really gone; as if he might answer if I call him. He stops where books are scattered on the ground. "Some of these are mine," he says, sifting through tattered, torn, and dusty covers.

The first thing he chooses to pick up, the thing he tries to salvage, is a book he finds from his destroyed library. It's an unabridged copy of *Gulliver's Travels*. He had read it a few times, I remember him telling me years ago. In vain he tries to knock off the dust and debris, but he carries it with him nonetheless. I think the loss of his library broke his heart in ways other losses had not. His books were the accumulation of his intellectual labor, years of reading, thinking, and journeying the world through the written word. Books were integral to his identity. His place in the world as a thinker, a teacher, a writer, was anchored to his library. To see it dismantled, discarded, and burned, I believe, turned off the lights in an unreachable part of him.

Over the years, Refaat and I had several discussions about his embrace of English literature instead of Arabic. Having been forced to leave my Arabic education at a young age, I would lament to him that it pained me to have never developed a sophisticated grasp of my poetically charged mother tongue. He agreed, mostly. But he found English more practical and pliable. More importantly, he wanted to master the language of the empire that oppressed him. Always thinking of Palestinian liberation, Refaat believed there was great value in speaking and writing to the people of empire to lay bare our humanity before them. He believed people were essentially good; that if they could only see what was happening to us, they would stop supporting our colonizers; that if they could see the magnificent beauty of our souls, they might love us. He also wanted to ensure our lives would be recorded despite rampant efforts to erase our presence in the world.

Still, he was uncompromising in his convictions, and never withheld the sting of his tongue against injustice. His integrity and dignity, and the dignity and agency of Palestinians on the whole, were above all else.

As tributes now poured in for Refaat, all our grief mixing together, his poem for Shymaa recited over and over by so many people around the world, I was reminded of another indigenous leader who, like Refaat, was murdered because the light of her being shone too brightly. Berta Cáceres of Honduras spent her life fighting for indigenous rights and for our deteriorating planet against extractive industries dismembering the earth, damming rivers, killing species, and stealing resources. When she died, the rallying cry of the thousands who loved and followed her was, "*Berta no murió, se multiplicó!*"

Likewise, *Refaat no murió, se multiplicó!*

Refaat did not die, he multiplied!

**susan abulhawa**
August 13, 2024

# Introduction

A son of Shujaiya, Refaat Alareer was born to a Palestinian family in Gaza on September 23, 1979. When he was eight years old, his hometown played a major role in the first Palestinian intifada (uprising), with residents leading protests and strikes alongside fierce clashes with Israeli occupation soldiers. Refaat spent his childhood creating and flying kites. As a young teenager, he threw stones at Israeli soldiers. He was shot and injured during these clashes, a secret that he kept until later in life.

Refaat's mission in life was not only to tell his story, but to empower others to tell theirs. He was a natural storyteller, a gift he credited to his grandmother Kamla and his mother Rifqa. His grandfather would bribe him with tea to stay by his side, but Refaat always preferred the stories of his grandmother. He often shared his mother's tale of surviving a near-death experience as a student in the 1960s, when Israeli forces attacked Shujaiya during a military raid. For Refaat, keeping memories alive was a matter of survival.

For this reason, he committed to telling stories to his children, people around him, and his students. One day, his little daughter Shymaa took him aback when she asked him: "Dad, who created the Jews?" Answering her question, Refaat returned to the importance of storytelling. Shymaa's use of the term "Jews" is common in Palestine to refer to Israeli Jews who came to Palestine as settlers, as religion was mostly the only unifying factor that brought them together. For Refaat, telling stories to Shymaa and her other siblings was his way of explaining history and the current reality in Gaza. Later, he asked his students at the English Department of the Islamic University of Gaza to write their stories about life under occupation. He later bragged that some of the students wrote phenomenally, even though it was their first time writing, and repeated his firm belief that all students have stories to tell. These stories were edited and eventually published in 2014 as an anthology titled *Gaza Writes Back*.

The success of *Gaza Writes Back*, including translations into numerous languages, encouraged Refaat to dedicate his life to training young people in narrative writing, storytelling, creative writing, and social media. He organized dozens of free courses and gave lectures in order to develop an army of young writers and bloggers able to challenge Israel's narrative on Palestine and convey their own experiences. Refaat believed that before Palestinians can live in a free Palestine, they have to create a free Palestine in their imagination through stories, films, novels, and the arts.

For Refaat, Palestine was a stone and a story away—a line he often repeated and used to sign copies of his book. After having planted the seeds of storytelling in his students, he then began telling stories of his own. He started a blog called, "In Gaza, My Gaza," where he published poems, articles, and memes. "If I Must Die," his most famous poem, first appeared on this blog in 2011. Since his killing, "If I Must Die" has served as Refaat's enduring testament to his students and followers around the world. Back in 2007, he set up Eye on Palestine, one of the first Palestinian websites where students could post in English.

This book is a reminder to keep Refaat's legacy alive. "If I Must Die" speaks to a man who loved life, who took pleasure in it, and at the same time, who treated seriously his life's mission as an educator for liberation. Refaat's life was unfairly cut short by his oppressors because he used his pen to debunk their lies. He deployed wisdom, intellect, and wit to make a mockery out of Israel's occupation and the fragile narratives it spread about Gaza. But if Israel believed that killing Refaat would extinguish his influence, it has been sorely disappointed. Refaat is now known to millions of people worldwide, who read his writings, watch his interviews, and fly kites on Gaza solidarity protests in tribute to his work. Refaat's message will ring eternal.

In class, Refaat did his best to open the minds and broaden the horizons of young people who had spent their entire lives confined behind Israeli fences. He educated students about Malcolm X and analyzed Palestinian literature as well as texts from international authors. Refaat was global in the classroom. He is now global in death, too. Refaat achieved an M.A. in Britain and a Ph.D. in Malaysia. He could have taught anywhere, but chose to return to

Gaza. He was an organic intellectual, down-to-earth, and loved deeply by his students. The adoration was mutual, as Refaat cared for his students like his own children. He financially supported some of his students by secretly buying them course books, wrote recommendation letters, and encouraged them to pursue personal development and higher education.

Refaat believed that for Palestinians to be able to connect with the rest of the world and tell their story, they must break the intellectual siege imposed on them by Israel that keeps Palestinians isolated. While motivating students to seek higher education around the world, he always encouraged them to return to Gaza. For him, the battle over narrative begins and ends there.

On December 6, 2023, Israel decided that it could no longer let Refaat write back from Gaza. A missile targeted Refaat in his sister's apartment, killing him along with his sister, brother, and four of his nephews and nieces. Some five months later, on April 26, 2024, an Israeli airstrike killed Refaat's beloved daughter, Shymaa, along with her husband and baby. Refaat loved the eulogy read at Malcolm X's funeral, part of which said: "Did you ever talk to Brother Malcolm? … Did you ever really listen to him? Did he ever do a mean thing? For if you did, you would know him. And if you knew him, you would know why we must honor him: Malcolm was our manhood, our living, black manhood!"

And now, we ask the same questions about brother Refaat. Did you ever talk to Brother Refaat? Did you ever have him smile at you? Did you ever really listen to him? For if you did, you would know him. And if you knew him, you would know why we must honor him. Refaat was our storyteller, our living prince, who never shied away from telling our story as it is, the story of a people under a brutal regime, who have been fighting for their freedom by any means necessary.

May the words of Refaat and his legacy bring us closer to freedom.

**Yousef M. Aljamal, editor**
A student and friend of Refaat Alareer
June 2024

"Writing in general is an obligation to ourselves and to humanity and to the future generations because it's usually the most important thing that we leave behind. And writing is the most important sort of understanding—when you speak to people you usually chose words randomly but when you write you think carefully what message you want to convey"

—2014

# A Modest Proposal

*December 22, 2010*

Two years ago the Israeli occupation leaders declared that a war against Hamas is to be waged as Hamas violates the conventions of combat by targeting "innocent" Israeli settlers/civilians. I can't deny that some rejoiced and giggled at this news. In the course of the conflict, about 1,500 Gazans fell and more than 4,000 were injured some of whom sustained permanent disability. In one wave of killing, the Israeli war planes targeted hundreds of Palestinians who were forced to leave their homes and take refuge in a school run by the UN thinking that would prevent Israel from targeting them. They were wrong. Forty of them were slain.

Has Israel really meant to target Hamas per se? Or has it meant any person/building/plant/blow of air/house/shop/mosque/field/nursery/motorbike and anything related to Hamas? Does that include places Hamas members passed by or [had] been in? Does that include people who happened to shake hands with a Hamas member, unknow-ingly perhaps? The facts on the ground tell that it is the Gazans Israel is after not Hamas. Of the five thousand casualties the majority are kids, women, elderly people, and police cadets. Only a handful of fighters fell during the fighting.

Now and in the light of these statistics, there must be a way out. And I have got a proposal. I shall now therefore humbly propose my own thoughts, which I hope will not be liable to the least objection. I, like the Israelis, believe there is a serious problem in Gaza with a great need for a solution. As far as Gaza is concerned, the problem does not lie in Hamas, but the problem with Gaza is that it is full of Gazans.

Why does not the Israeli government buy/kidnap/arrest (or use any available means) Gazans and eat them? If put to action, this proposal will have several different advantages: Israel satisfies its cannibalistic desires, quenches its blood thirst, rids itself of Gazans, and saves a lot of money and ammunitions for wars to come. In addition, the carcasses can be used to help Israelis build a wall all around Gaza.

A modest proposal, ain't [it]?

"The problem with Gaza is that it is full of Gazans"

—2010

# Israel's Power of the Camera: Gaza's Power of Gaza

*December 22, 2010*

The Gaza Crisis in Gaza is no crisis. The poverty of Gazans is not poverty, their ailment is not an ailment, and their need is not a need. Everyone in Gaza is living happily. Gazans whose houses were bombarded by the Israeli war machine and could not build new ones due to the Israeli tightened siege do not sleep in ragged tents under the clear skies of Gaza, clear sky if you do not account for the Israeli drones and warplanes. And those tents are first class: in the summer mosquitoes can't get in from the holes made by the sun shining on them for the past two years, no, neither water in the winter. For Israel's propaganda machine, Gaza is the "Roots," a fancy restaurant that serves very expensive meals that even some Israelis can't afford. The Roots, though very few Gazans know it or ever heard of it, is the destination of hundreds of thousands of Gazans who love to throw fifty bucks on a meal. Seventy percent of the people in Gaza, for the Israelis, do not live under the poverty line but are soaked in sumptuousness and comfort. That the majority of Gaza people live on a dollar a day is a viciously fabricated lie.

In the previous aggressive election (I mean military) campaign on Gazans, Israel did not kill 1,500 Palestinians. It certainly did not destroy hundreds of houses and for sure did not injure thousands. The Israeli Camera and IDF official clips showed us the trucks loaded with humanitarian aid allowed, by Israel, into the Gaza Strip. We saw pictures and videos of the Israeli warships targeting places they claimed were weapon caches. Although the clips had so many cuts and so many big question marks about their authenticity, the Israelis as well as peoples of the world are fooled into taking them for granted. For the Israelis, Gaza was floating on weapons. One clip on YouTube shows an Israeli missile targeting a gas tank. In the aftermath of the explosion fire erupts. That is taken as a clear-cut proof. The target was a weapon store. Period. The clip soon hits over two hundred thousand views and ZERO comments. IDF desk has disabled comments. No one has to ask why the IDF YouTube channel disabled the comments. Just take it as it is served to you. And say Amen.

The Israeli hermetic seal imposed on the Strip for the past four years is not a siege. It is self-defense. This act of self-defense, guaranteed by international law, enabled Israel to deprive everything and everybody of the main traits they possess. Students can't travel to study abroad, fishermen can't fish, farmers can't farm, teachers can't teach, merchants are not allowed to engage in trade, businessmen do no Business, Gazans can't live in Gaza. And what is their reason. We are Gazans?

"When [my students] get to break the walls of isolation the occupation and Egypt are creating, when they meet Jewish people who are working for our cause, it's going to make all the difference"

—2014

# Tragedy in One Sentence

*January 21, 2011*

Oblivious to the likely new happenings around her, unable to fully grasp the faintest idea of the reason why not only all her relatives and beloved ones but also every Tom, Dick, and Harry, even that hateful one-eyed shopkeeper, was there gathering in the tiny ragged tent, newly erected by little boys she only saw their look-alikes on TV hurling stones at something she could not form a complete image of as it used to pass those kids so quickly that they, dodging low to evade live bullets but not too low to miss the target, had to throw their stones perhaps ten seconds before to make sure they hit it, seeing masked grown-ups covering the walls of her house with graffiti, feeling proud, a sense of finally belonging to whatever was going on around her, and she, of course, being unable to fathom what they are, a sense she longed for for ages because her first grader classmate, Heba, used to tease her that unlike the walls of Heba's house, hers were, to quote Heba, "as white as snow," something bad in itself in a culture that values any kind of resistance even if it is a slogan scribbled on the walls of their houses by a boy whose chicken scratch can be read by none but Champollion himself, going back home that afternoon to check on her mother, a plump young lady in her mid-twenties who had to marry early as she was left orphan by an Israeli shell that destroyed their house and killed all her family members except her who happened to be sleeping over at her cousin, whose elder brother married her seven years later more out of pity than passion, and now having to bear the awful harshness of going on through life with a husband buried two meters beneath with a Palestinian flag waving over his grave and a smiling picture on the headstone and on the walls of the neighborhood waiting there not for the occupation to tear them down under their heavy boots but by killing another yet young, full-of-life person whose pictures will cover that of her husband, nothing but pictures of martyrs can cover the faces of other martyrs in Palestine, having now to bring a dozen of kids, the oldest of whom was approaching her with quizzical glances wondering what was going on, the mother trying to hide her emotions, smiled slightly, dragged her daughter not closer to her heart lest should the little one hear the deafening screams of the broken heart, unaware, again, that from now on she will be labelled an orphan, the little girl seeing her mother smiling, slept in her lap to be awakened minutes later by the bitter crying of her Mom, who, though trying to suppress her inner torture and agony yet failing to keep calm the moment her little daughter while asleep called for her dad not once but thrice, with her high-pitched wailing, caused her confused daughter to cry uncontrollably.

"I want my children to plan, rather than worry about, their future, and to draw beaches or fields of blue skies and a sun in the corner, not warships, pillars of smoke, warplanes, and guns"

—2014

# Gaza Mourns Vittorio Arrigoni

*April 15, 2011*

I do not know Vittorio Arrigoni in person, but my tears
and heart do.* Thousands of Gazans cried over his tragic
and untimely death. Many, appalled by the crime, are still
trying to make sense of what happened. Nothing makes
sense. It was a murder that shocked Gaza. One glance
at google pictures will show that this courageous man
not only was very pro-Palestinian but also was helping
Palestinians more than we Palestinians can help ourselves.
Who in Gaza would not mourn the man who we saw on
every boat and every vessel defying Israeli naval siege?
Who did not see Vittorio participating in popular protests

---

*\*Editor's note:* Vittorio Arrigoni (1975–2011) was an Italian writer and
activist with the International Solidarity Movement. In 2011, Arrigoni
was killed in Gaza by a group affiliated with al-Qaeda.

against Israeli buffer zones near Gaza borders? How many of us, Palestinians, held a Palestinian flag protesting Israeli occupation and inhumane measures against us? Vittorio did. Who did not cross his or her fingers when he was kidnapped by the Israeli navy and injured by the Israeli occupation forces for helping the people of Gaza? One word only was repeated in the previous questions: Israel. Yes, the Israeli occupation is the only party benefiting from the wilful murder of this freedom activist.

The timing, which comes days before Flotilla II,* and the irreparable damage the crime did to Gaza and the Palestinians tell of the Israeli Mossad hand lurking behind the doers. For Israel, the best way to prevent a second encounter with a freedom fleet is to scare the participants away. Imagine how many people will either in fear or in protest stop joining the flotilla. But that is a secondary issue now, for Vittorio is gone. Also imagine how many articles will be written to prove that the people of Gaza are a bunch of bigots who do not deserve a helping hand let alone sacrificing one's life for. But does that matter? For Vittorio is no more. Imagine how much damage this act of barbarity does to the image of Gaza. Yet that is not the concern, for Vittorio is dead.

Gaza alone will pay for the premature death of comrade Vittorio. Gaza alone will suffer the dire consequences.

---

*Editor's note:* In 2011, an international "Freedom Flotilla" was planned to break Israel's illegal maritime blockade of Gaza.

Gaza alone will have to bear the responsibility. The question every Gazan is asking now is what have those people who did this done to resist the Israeli occupation? Nil, zilch, nada, nothing. Does not that cast doubt on their agendas and goals; while they caused the death of many Palestinians, the Israeli occupation remains and untouched by this handful of extremists.

But still could the murderers have done it? They did. Did they plan it themselves? I doubt it. Vittorio's death means one thing: the death sentence for the killers. The clash between this group and the Hamas government in 2008 proves that Hamas will not have mercy upon anyone who tries to disturb the (already shaken) security of Gaza. They have learnt the lesson the hard way. And another stupid mistake like killing an innocent Italian activist who left his home and family behind to help is the final blow for those people. Everyone in Gaza knows that. And the criminals do too. By so doing, they are either too stupid to see their end coming or so blinded that they were tricked into a mistake that will be their last.

The only people smiling now are the Israeli politicians and Mossad agents. But we say to the world that there is a huge difference between Palestinians and Israel. The killings of foreign journalists and activists by Israel were both systematic and premeditated and done by the Israeli army establishment. No one was brought to justice. In Gaza, the doers of this shameful event are very few and do not represent the Palestinian people. And we are sure they will be brought to justice and punished accordingly. Or else we will be like the rogue state of Israel. No one can forget Israel's long history of killing and attacking journalists and peace activists such as Rachel Corrie, James Miller, Raffaele Ciriello, the flotilla activists, and others.

Now as Gazans and friends of Vittorio Arrigoni, we demand the government of Gaza to:

1. Bring the doers to justice and punish them. And yes, we use the death penalty in Gaza.

2. Apologize to his family and the Italian people on behalf of the people of Palestine.

3. Name a street after Vittorio.

4. Name a school after him.

5. Declare a day of mourning.

6. Grant Vittorio a Palestinian nationality.

While that will show how much we care and how much Vittorio means to Gazans, it will not compensate us or his family or his friends for the loss of a great man, a man who stood bare-chested in front of the Israeli machine guns, a man who was beaten and arrested by Israelis for the sake of Gaza, a man who loved Gaza and whom Gaza will never forget.

Vittorio Arrigoni, we are sorry. Italy, we are sorry. Italians, we are sorry. Free people of the world, Gaza is sorry.

Everyone will make sure this thing does not happen again. We won't rest until those criminals are brought to justice. And we promise not to let a handful of misguided fanatics determine the future and destiny of Gaza until Gaza is free.

# If I Must Die, Let It Be a Tale

If I must die,

you must live

to tell my story

to sell my things

to buy a piece of cloth

and some strings,

(make it white with a long tail)

so that a child, somewhere in Gaza

while looking heaven in the eye

awaiting his dad who left in a blaze—

and bid no one farewell

not even to his flesh

not even to himself—

sees the kite, my kite you made, flying up above

and thinks for a moment an angel is there

bringing back love

If I must die

let it bring hope

let it be a tale

*November 27, 2011*

# I Was Mustafa Tamimi

*December 12, 2011*

Fifteen years ago I was Mustafa Tamimi.* Two months before that it was a relative who had his skull smashed by an explosive bullet from an Israeli sniper. Later that same week another neighbor lost his eye. Before and since then, the same situation has been repeating itself again and again: an armored jeep, a soldier armed to teeth, a tiny figure of mere flesh and bones, and a stone smeared with blood on the side of the road. That's the saga of Palestine. That's our tale, full of injustice and oppression, whose hero struts and frets and whoever gets in his way is doomed. But we get in his way anyway.

---

*Editor's note:* On December 9, 2011, Israeli soldiers in the West Bank fired a tear gas canister at Mustafa Tamimi from close range. The canister struck Tamimi in the face; he died from his injuries the following day. Tamimi was twenty-eight years old when he was killed.

The pain the two rubber-coated bullets caused I can't feel now. They do not hurt. But the grinning face of the Rambo-like Israeli soldier still does. I was mature enough then to realize that those were enemies, our enemies who are messing up everything in our lives. (I did not need anyone to teach me that by the way because I have eyes that see and ears that hear.) Never had I thought then that those soldiers were sometimes doing the occupation thing for "merry sport." Despite the glaring gazes, the frowns that left their faces wrinkled and the beatings some of my friends and I had for just being there, I had the impression that the Israeli soldiers who hit a Palestinian boy spent their nights mooning about what they did. They apparently did not. And that grin was the proof. And Mustafa Tamimi's the most recent walking (had not he been put down) evidence.

*Yet, I blame Mustafa.*

Yes, he is to blame. He is to blame for believing deep in his heart that those trigger-happy soldiers may not shoot directly at him and if they do they might not shoot to kill. He is to blame for not armoring his body with shields of steel. He is to blame for fighting for his rights. Ten thousand dead Palestinians in the past ten years or so prove without doubt that when Israeli soldiers shoot they shoot to kill and when they aim, they aim to hit. And yet again, not once have we heard of a Palestinian quitting his struggle for independence and human rights for that reason. Instead, anger, protests, resistance, and determination would grow day by day and hour by hour.

In doing so, Israel seems to be pushing the Palestinians yet again toward a corner whose options are very limited and whose consequences might be devastatingly harmful for both sides

*No peaceful protests. So?*

Israel's aggression against the peaceful protesters in the West Bank (particularly in Ni'lin, Bi'lin, and Nabi Saleh) that culminated in the killing of Mustafa Tamimi is but a powerful expression of Israel's policy: even peaceful demos are not welcome and are to be met with force and fire. That obviously leaves the doors wide open for Palestinians to think of other possible ways to inflict pain as a reaction to the barbarity of an army that insists on turning a deaf ear to the pleas of the people whose lands, and fields, and properties, and houses are being destroyed and/or seized and confiscated forever. That rings a bell?

That reminds us of the projectiles of the first and the second intifada.

The Palestinian intifadas did not start one day out of the blue with the next day Palestinian resistance groups throwing homemade rockets at settlements and Israeli towns. Ten years ago not one single Palestinian (not even those with the wildest imagination) could have foreseen that certain kinds of rockets will be used in the struggle. But Israel made it possible. By crushing stone throwers, Israel was, albeit not directly, saying to the Palestinians, "you better think of other weapons." And Palestinians did.

Therefore, the two intifadas developed not according to the laws of necessity and inevitability or in regards to a certain theory of evolution: a stone, a Molotov cocktail, a gun, and then homemade rockets. Israel developed it. As we were throwing stones, thinking that would deter and curb the ills and evils of the occupation, Israel was growing fiercer and fiercer: evolving from shooting to injure, to Rabin's bone-smashing policy, to shooting to kill, to collective destruction, to mass killings.

A third intifada is looming in the horizon, I believe. We can see it in the sparks coming out of the barrels of Israeli automatic guns. We can see it in the lifeless, yet full of life, body of Mustafa Tamimi. We can see it in the grins of the soldiers, who, while shooting at Palestinians, intend to kill. It is Israel that is making the third intifada inevitable.

# Mustafa's Only Care

A chap
A stone
A kuffiya
A will and a fist.

*

The jeep
The soldier
His guns and powder
His mask
His elbows, knees and helmet.

*

A hamlet.

*

And People run
And pull and push
And come and go.
And people fall
And rise and fall.

*

"RUN! RUN! RUN!"

*

Yet, Mustafa does not care
And he does not scare
Because he cares!

*

"Shoot to kill!
Damn it!"
And then they fall
And fall and fall.
And Mustafa rises
And lights the way

*

And people run
And pull and push
And come and come.
They rise and rise
For Mustafa cares

*

*This poem is inspired by Mustafa Tamimi, whose untimely death at the hands of Israeli soldiers showed the light to many people to come.*

*Rest in Peace, brother.*

*December 11, 2011*

# On a Drop of Rain

*2014*

Scientists still do not unanimously agree whether raindrops originate in the sky as ice crystals or not. But that does not matter to me. I am no scientist.

Abu Samy is a Palestinian farmer from the West Bank. He was busy on that windy day weeding his field—or what was left of it. He regretted not listening to his wife's frequent pleas not to go out. He was always doubtful about what she calls her "special gift," her "sense of the rain." He never listened to her, and if he did, he did not pay attention to her interpretations and elaboration of her different methods of skillfully and accurately predicting when it will or will not rain, for how long, and how heavy the rain will be. Although she must have told him the very same tale hundreds of times, he cannot retell her explanation except in excerpts. Um Samy touches the earth. She holds a tiny grain of sand, whispers to it, and listens back. In cases when communication fails, she smells the grain. But that is metaphorically speaking. At least Abu Samy thinks so.

On the southern side of the Wall, Abu Samy, along with thousands of Palestinian farmers, is not allowed to build rooms or erect tents, lest they should use these tents or structures to dig tunnels to the Israeli side. At least Abu Samy is luckier than his fellow farmers; he lost only two thirds of his land. Countless others of his friends and relatives had their fields swallowed by the Israeli Wall cutting through the lands of the West Bank. For Abu Samy at this very moment, the wall was useful. Living under occupation has taught him to see hope in the darkest of tunnels—not that he digs such tunnels to infiltrate into the Israeli side. He ran to the Wall. Gluing himself to the lengthy expanse of concrete, he was shielded from the heavy rain and the strong wind, though only partially, by the Wall.

On the other side of the Wall stood an Israeli farmer whose wife, too, had predicted rain (and warned him against Palestinians infiltrating the security fence). He wanted to run to the concrete room he built a couple of weeks ago, but as the Wall was closer, he hurried toward it. If they both had listened carefully, Abu Samy and the Israeli farmer would have heard their hearts beating against the Wall. Or maybe they did hear the heartbeats but mistook them for the rumble of distant thunder.

It was one particular drop of rain, a very tiny one. It could have fallen on Abu Samy's bare head had it not been for a sudden gust of wind that pushed it to the other side of the

Wall; it fell on the Israeli farmer's helmet. He never felt it.

Other drops, however, were racing toward and seemingly preferring the unshielded head of Abu Samy.

That drops of rain begin their existence as ice crystals seems, to Abu Samy, very possible. But who cares about Abu Samy's views. He is Palestinian.

# O, Earth
# (Land Day Poem)

Hug me

And hold me tight

Or devour me

To suffer no more.

I love thee

So take me.

Make me rich.

Make me dirt.

Gone are the days of serenity. .

Guns are the words of humanity.

I have no food but a thorn,

No sport but a sigh.

For a soldier needs to feel high.

O, Earth,

If in life I am to hurt

Let my dirt in you give birth.

**O, Earth.**

*January 16, 2012*

# Narrating Palestine

## *2014*

More than five years ago, during Israel's 2008–2009 twenty-three-day large-scale offensive war on Gaza, Operation Cast Lead, my little daughter, Shymaa, who was only five years old, asked me and my wife a question that still puzzles me, as on several occasions it has become my own. Amidst the sounds of explosions and the smell of gunpowder, her question, in her soft, shaky voice, came as a shock to both of us. "Who created the Jews?" she asked, looking me in the eyes and then turning to her mother in anticipation of an answer. For a while, neither of us was able to talk, let alone answer her question. Bemused, I offered to tell her a story, and several other stories followed.

If I could not answer her question, one thing I did know was why Shymaa, in the space of a few weeks, had grown up enough to ask such a profound question. She must have thought that the merciful and loving God she learns about in her kindergarten, who usually saves the good guys in her mother's stories, could not be the same God who created those killing machines that for long days and nights brought us nothing but death, chaos, destruction, tears, pain, and fear, causing her and her little brothers to wake up at night and sob hysterically. Her version of God could not be the creator of the same people who caused our windows to shatter and who, two days earlier, shot at her father when I was filling water tanks on the roof of our house during the two-hour ceasefire.

Israel's Operation Cast Lead murdered more than 1,400 Palestinians and injured thousands, most of whom were children, women, and elderly people. Many of the injured are now disabled for life, and many of the martyrs left children and wives orphaned and widowed for life. Five years ago, Israel destroyed more than six thousand housing units. More than twenty thousand Palestinians were made homeless, some forcibly displaced for the fourth or fifth time in their lives. The war came after a long siege that Israel is still imposing on Gaza, a siege that has left almost all aspects of life paralyzed. Israel targeted infrastructure, schools, universities, factories, houses, and fields. Everyone was a possible target. Every house could be turned into wreckage in a split second. There was no right time or right place in Gaza. The whole of Gaza was the bull's-eye for Israel's most sophisticated military arsenal. It was clear as crystal to Gazans then that Israel was deliberately and systematically targeting life and hope, and that Israel wanted to make sure that after the offensive we had nothing of either to cling to, and that we are silenced forever.

## Telling stories

The five years that followed Operation Cast Lead were the most productive years of my life. As a young adult man with an M.A. degree from University College London, teaching world literature and creative writing at the Islamic University in Gaza, I had great opportunities to be part of the struggle for Palestinian national rights. My job gave me the chance to work with some of the most brilliant students in Palestine, many of whom contributed to *Gaza Writes Back*, the anthology of short stories I was to spend over a year editing, to showcase Palestinian creative resistance to injustice and to Israeli racism and brutality. But how I got there requires a story about coming to understand the significance of stories.

I remember vividly how I spent the twenty-three days preparing for the second semester, because I believed there would be life after the offensive. I was rereading Daniel Defoe's *Robinson Crusoe*. And for the first time, it dawned on me how Friday's story was mediated by a self-appointed, colonial, supremacist master assuming ownership of a land that was not his. Crusoe's imperialist discourse had never before annoyed me like it did then—"My island was now peopled, and I thought myself very rich in subjects . . . my people were perfectly subjected. I was absolute lord and lawgiver, they all owed their lives to me, and were ready to lay down their lives." I thought there had to be a different story that Friday could have told, had he not been silenced, and that we Palestinians should never be the Man Friday of anyone—that we have to own our own narrative, and that no one but us can better reveal the sheer pain and suffering we are made to experience. If Israel's apartheid has to be fought, Israel's narratives have to be challenged, and exposed.

It was then that I realized much of my mother's wisdom. For years, she told me and my siblings many stories. And many a time, I gave my mother a grumpy how-many-more-times-are-you-going-to-tell-this-same-story face as she retold the same story, again and again. In response, my mother, who gave birth to fourteen of us—eight boys and six girls, me being the second eldest—started experimenting with the stories, not only by adding new interesting details, but also by zooming in and out as she saw fit, to serve her purposes. The stories became more engaging. My mom, through this rare act of compromise, must have realized that the purposes of telling us stories are a lot more important than simply keeping us quiet or even correcting our bad behaviors, like making us eat vegetables because the boy in the story who did not eat was easily carried away by a giant fly. (I cannot help but remember Mom's story about the lazy boy whose mother asked him to go out and see if it was raining. The boy replied, "OK, when the cat comes in, I will feel its hair and see if it is wet!") My usually multi-tasking mother dedicated her everything to the story when she was telling one. The story appeared on her facial expressions, in her tone of voice, and through her gestures, and added solemnity to her already radiant face. My mother believed in her stories. And my mother's stories became and still are part of our lives. It was only later in life that I realized my mother's strong belief in the power of stories, and understood that there are several ways to tell the very same thing. Sometimes my mother asked us to tell our own stories or even to repeat one of hers. The stories gave my mother more authority and power; single voices, my mother must have believed, are blindly dangerous. As children living in the first intifada, for us the stories of my mother and those of my grandparents were our solace, our escort in a blind world controlled by soldiers and guns and death. In part, they are responsible for the person I am today, although very few might have predicted that the reckless stone-thrower of the first intifada would grow up to be an academic at university.

Despite the attacks, or rather more accurately because of them, I found myself telling my three kids, Shymaa, Omar, and Ahmed, either the same stories Mom told me, or different stories with similar themes, featuring my children as the heroes and saviors every now and then. Nothing broke the concentration except the intermittent "Boom! Boom!" sounds. That was how I spent most of the time, trying to make sure I was in the room least likely to take a hit from Israeli stray(!) missiles. The stories I told my kids and my brother's kids, who crowded the place and helped make the cold room warmer with their breath, were not mere pastime pleasures, nor were they prepared in a scholarly way. They just came out. Stories in Palestine just come out. You decide to tell stories and the stories just appear. The characters start to gather and then everything, to the amazement of the storyteller, unfolds. If charity begins at home, so too do stories. As a Palestinian, I have been brought up on stories and storytelling. It's both selfish and treacherous to keep a story to yourself—stories are meant to be told and retold. If I allowed a story to stop, I would be betraying my legacy, my mother, my grandmother, and my homeland. To me, storytelling is one of the ingredients of Palestinian *sumud*—steadfastness. Stories teach life even if the hero suffers or dies at the end. For Palestinians, stories whet the much-needed talent for life.

*Gaza Writes Back*

In the immediate aftermath of the Israeli operation, when we dusted ourselves off from the most immediate pain and agony that came with Cast Lead, Gaza went back to normal, only this time there were piles of bodies, houses, orphans, ruins, and stories to tell. I went back to my classrooms and to my students at the English Department of the Islamic University in Gaza, which had its newest, highly equipped laboratory building bombarded by Israel. Scars were everywhere. Every single person in Gaza had to mourn a loved one. I started inviting my friends and students to write about what they had endured and to bear witness to the anguish the operation had caused. "Writing is a testimony," I told them, "a memory that outlives any human experience, and an obligation to communicate with ourselves and the world. We lived for a reason, to tell the tales of loss, of survival, and of hope."

The plan was to start writing personal experience, nonfiction creative pieces, and then transform our writing to fiction. Writing creative pieces was new to many of my students, let alone writing short fiction. Some initially resisted, and it was only when they started believing in themselves and their unique position in history, and came to understand that storytelling is a creative act of resistance to oppression, that they started writing. For they eventually can become voices of their generation. Stories and articles started pouring out. If storytelling is significant to us as Palestinians, then writing these stories is of paramount importance. It was high time to break the intellectual embargo Israel has been enforcing for decades, and similarly, it was high time to break with psychological shackles and talk to non-Arabs in the language and discourse they understand.

Three years after Operation Cast Lead, I collected tens of creative pieces written by my students and friends. I started using some of them in my creative writing and literature classes as samples to show the students that they too can write. The more stories I collected, the more I believed they had to be published in a book. When I was approached, then, by Just World Books to curate a book out of the pieces on my personal blog, I suggested a short story collection instead. When I called for submissions at university campuses in Gaza and on Facebook and Twitter, I received dozens more stories. They struck me with their diversity and maturity. What I wanted, however, was twenty-three stories in order to counterattack the twenty-three days of terror in Operation Cast Lead. I wanted stories to represent life in the face of death, hope in the face of despair, and selflessness in the face of horrible selfishness. The twenty-three short stories chosen for *Gaza Writes Back* testify against one of the most brutal occupations the world has known. I saw in the stories the potential for bringing together a range of Palestinian voices into one book. The stories endeavor to educate both Palestinians and a wider audience, because these young writers strongly believe there is still a lot to share and because we believe it is our moral obligation to educate the world about our plight and travails as Palestinians living under Israeli occupation. *Gaza Writes Back* does not give voice to Palestinians. Palestinians have their own voices. Rather, *Gaza Writes Back* showcases some of these Palestinian voices. These stories are acts of resistance and defiance, proclaiming the endurance of Palestinians and the continuing resilience and creativity of our culture in the face of ongoing obstacles and attempts to silence us.

*Palestine is a story away!*

In Palestine, no family gathering lacks stories of those good old days when Palestine was the Palestine that current generations have not experienced directly. Because of this storytelling, there is a Palestine that dwells inside all of us, a Palestine that needs to be revived: a free Palestine where all people regardless of color, religion, or race coexist; a Palestine where the meaning of the word "occupation" no longer connotes the death, destruction, pain, suffering, deprivation, isolation, and restrictions that Israel has injected into this word. These horrendous Israeli practices, and many others, are ones young Palestinian writers capture in literary forms in search of their Palestine. While sometimes portrayed metaphorically, Palestine can be a beautiful reality. Palestine is a martyr away, a tear away, a missile away, or a whimper away. Palestine is a story away.

While *Gaza Writes Back* contests negative narratives propagated by Israel about Palestine, that is not the only reason for its existence. Writing is an act not only of preserving history and human experience, but also of resistance to intruders and colonizers. Although we do not write only because there is occupation and injustice, we write the kind of literature we do because there is occupation. Like any other people who have lived under ruthless occupation, as Palestinians we believe in Chinua Achebe's powerful statement:

> Then I grew older and began to read about adventures in which I didn't know that I was supposed to be on the side of those savages who were encountered by the good white man. I instinctively took sides with the white people. They were fine! They were excellent. They were intelligent. The others were not . . . they were stupid and ugly. That was the way I was introduced to the danger of not having your own stories. There is that great proverb—that until the lions have their own historians, the history of the hunt will always glorify the hunter. That did not come to me until much later. Once I realized that, I had to be a writer. I had to be that historian. It's not one man's job. It's not one person's job. But it is something we have to do, so that the story of the hunt will also reflect the agony, the travail—the bravery, even, of the lions.

We know we belong here in Palestine. We write not to beg for our rights and for a better life, but to fulfill our obligations to ourselves, to others, and to the generations to come. And in so many ways, the struggle in Palestine for land and rights has been fought metaphorically and verbally. Even the colonization of Palestine came in the form of a poem and a story long before it became a reality. Hence, let a free Palestine materialize first in the form of a story or a poem. *Gaza Writes Back* is a weapon to shatter the Israeli narratives of a land without a people, of a people without roots, a people who never existed and never will— through this writing, we not only assert our existence, but also envision our future.

*Five years later . . .*

*Gaza Writes Back* proves that sometimes a homeland becomes a story. We love the story because it is about our homeland and we love our homeland even more because of the story. And now, five years later, Israel continues its inhuman policies against Palestinians. And every time Israel escalates its violence—every time the Israeli government violates a truce, or murders someone, or jams the TV signal through its drones, or sends in F16s for casual sonic booms—I see the very same question in the eyes of my daughter, Shymaa. Five years have passed since Cast Lead, and Israel has not given me the slightest chance to explain that we all have the same God, or to see an end to all this crazy, man-made violence and evil in our midst that will stop when Israel ends its occupation and brutality against non-Jews.

Five years later, *Gaza Writes Back* took me and several Palestinian contributors to the US, where I met Palestinian and pro-Palestinian activists, some of whom were Jews. The tour, jointly sponsored by the book's publisher, Just World Books, and by the American Friends Service Committee, lasted from March 27 to April 24, 2014, and was aimed at promoting young Palestinian voices and empowering the Palestinian narrative. Although Sara Ali was denied permission by the Israeli government to join us from Gaza, I toured with Yousef Aljamal and Rawan Yaghi, who like me are currently seeking education outside Gaza. During our tour, we spoke in more than ten US cities in seven states, and met Palestinians living in the Diaspora, many of them born and raised in America. We also met hundreds of pro-Palestinian American activists; and most importantly, anti-Zionist Jewish activists working for justice in Palestine. We met with very promising young people from an African American organization in Chicago, who told us about US police brutality against Americans of color and the often-invisible wall of racism they still have to deal with. Hundreds of people from all walks of life came to listen to the young voices from Palestine, in churches, synagogues, bookstores, and houses. And we spoke about politics, literature, life, food, water, resistance, the future, racism, feminism, and justice. The tour was proof that fiction is universal, and that literature breaks barriers and returns us all to our humanity, which is, in Edward Said's words, "the only and I would go so far as saying the final resistance we have against the inhuman practices and injustices that disfigure human history."

Because of our travels, I now am able to tell my daughter Shymaa that not only have we been exposed to occupation and oppression, but we also have been subjected to isolation and segregation. I will tell her that we were made to believe the fight is between Jews and Palestinian Christians and Muslims. And I will tell her Israel builds walls and checkpoints to maintain this fiction and to keep us isolated. I will tell her that in my tour I learned that Jews, too, can and have been victims, and that Judaism has been hijacked by Zionism. I will tell Shymaa that we Palestinians still need to grow and keep gaining additional perspectives because the fight for Palestine is universal, and needs to be fought globally as well as nationally. In *The Battle for Justice in Palestine*, Ali Abunimah summarizes this understanding: "the struggle for Palestinian human rights must be closely linked to the struggle for human rights in the United States and around the world."

Now when I tell my daughter stories, I usually have in mind the generous Jewish hosts in Atlanta, whose five-year-old sweet daughter, Viola, kept asking me about optical illusions. I never gave Viola an answer to her question, because every time she asked it, my mind went to Shymaa, wishing she and the hundreds of thousands of Palestinian children had not been deprived by Israel of their right to live a decent life. Sometimes I think we may one day find it in our hearts to forgive Israeli leaders (when, among other things, occupation ends, apartheid is abolished, justice prevails, equal rights are guaranteed to all, refugees return, and reparations are made), but I do not think we will ever forgive them for not allowing our children to live a normal life, to ask about optical illusions rather than who was killed and why and whether that noise was an Israeli bomb or a resistance rocket. I want my children to plan, rather than worry about, their future, and to draw beaches or fields of blue skies and a sun in the corner, not warships, pillars of smoke, warplanes, and guns. Hopefully, the stories of *Gaza Writes Back* will help bring my daughter Shymaa and Viola together and give them consolation and solace to continue the struggle until Palestine is free. Until then, I will continue telling her stories.

"Israel wants us to be closed, isolated—
to push us to the extreme. It doesn't
want us to be educated. It doesn't
want us to see ourselves as part of a
universal struggle against oppression.
They don't want us to be educated or
to be educators"

—2014

# The Story of My Brother, Martyr Mohammed Alareer

*July 28, 2014*

My brother Mohammed Alareer, thirty-one, a father of two, was killed by an Israeli airstrike while he was at home. While he was at home.

No one knows yet if he bled for three days or if he died of the shockwaves from the explosion, or the sound, or the debris, or the shrapnel, or the fire or by them all.

But my brother Mohammed is gone.

His two very beautiful children, Raneem, four, and one-year-old Hamza, are without a father forever. And our big house of seven flats is gone.

A house of four floors but thousands of stories is no more.

The stories, however, will live to bear witness to the most brutally wild occupation the world has ever known.

*Hamada*

I am the second of fourteen children. Mohammed is number five after three boys and one girl. Of all my early memories in life, the birth of Mohammed is the most vivid. I was only four then.

When I heard they wanted to name my new brother Mohammed, I started crying and shouting, "I don't want you to name him Mohammed. I want you to name him Hamada! I want Hamada!"

I used to scream my lungs out every time someone called him Mohammed until no one dared do so. He was then known to all as Hamada (which is a pet name for Mohammed). Everyone called him Hamada except, to my disappointment, my dad, who always used his official name, Mohammed.

Ever since, I felt a very strong connection toward Hamada. It was like he was my son, like I owned him, like I had to take care of him and to make sure his name remained Hamada.

Born in 1983, Hamada was timid but humorous and adventurous. He would be silent most of the time, but when he did speak, he was usually seeking to go beyond the boundaries of the given.

The second intifada in the early 2000s gave him his real,

life-changing experiences as some of his school friends were killed by Israel and he took leading roles in their funeral processions.

Hamada went to college and finished a two-year degree in public relations, which equipped him with skills to reach out to people. At the beginning of the second intifada, in a matter of two years, people from all over the Gaza Strip started asking me if Hamada was my brother.

Surprised, I would smile and nod. And in my mind I would wonder what made him rise to fame. I realized later that my shy brother had started leading demonstrations and reciting poetic chants to mobilize the masses protesting an Israeli attack on Jerusalem, or he would lead nationalistic chants at the many funerals of martyrs we had in Shujaiya (locally, we pronounce it "Shijaiya") and elsewhere.

## Creative

Of all our fourteen brothers and sisters, Hamada was the most distinguished and creative. As he began his twenties, he became a totally different person, with many friends and many connections. As he became more outgoing, he also became even more creative and proactive.

Every time he told us about what he was doing, I would think of shy little Hamada who never looked at a camera until he was a teenager.

His newly developed public speaking and acting skills won him the role of Karkour, the most famous television character in the Gaza Strip. Karkour, a mischievous chicken, was the star of al-Aqsa TV's program *Tomorrow's Pioneers*, which hosted children from all over the Gaza Strip.

Hamada's character attracted an audience from all over Palestine and even the Arab world, where kids would call to protest Karkour's jaywalking, shouting over the telephone and other such annoying behaviors, and suggest to him more well-behaved alternatives.

Early this year, Hamada won a small role in another TV show that started airing this Ramadan but was stopped due to the ongoing Israeli onslaught.

The death of my brother will come as a shock to the large numbers of children whose favorite part of Friday was watching Karkour misbehave and helping him change into a better Karkour, thanks to their advice, only for him to relapse at the start of the next episode into another anti-social behavior.

By killing my brother, Israel has surely has killed a promising talent, and deprived thousands of children of a funny and educational program.

*Martyr number 26*

Hamada got married five years ago and had two children, Raneem and Hamza. And everyone, his wife and kids included, still called him Hamada. He was still living in my parents' place after he got married; he worked very hard to build his own flat in the same building, which he finished last year.

He was never able to move up to it, however, because the siege on Gaza, which became even tighter over the past year, made it very difficult for him to furnish the apartment.

Like all Palestinian victims who fell to Israeli terror and aggression, Hamada leaves behind a loving family. My brother will be martyr number 26 in my extended family; five of them were killed last week and had their bodies dug out of the rubble during Saturday's twelve-hour "humanitarian ceasefire."

When I spoke to my mother, who lost two nephews years ago, she was stronger than I ever imagined. My father was calmer than ever before.

They both told me about the tremendous destruction Israel left in Shijaiya—whose name means "the land of the brave." They told me about the families that lost five, ten, and even twenty members.

*"We are steadfast"*

Hearing my parents' reaction, I breathed a sigh of relief. I know how devastating it will be for them to lose a dear son. But their resilience, among so many other bereaved families, did not come as a surprise to me.

When I heard about the twelve-hour lull, I was afraid people, seeing the total destruction Israel left everywhere, would be shocked and give up their support for resistance, undoubtedly a goal of Israel's merciless attack. But I was wrong.

Israel intended to bomb people to surrender by randomly destroying houses and killing people in the streets. But to the contrary, what Israel's actions are doing is bringing Palestinians in Gaza to a position of "we have nothing to lose."

"We are patient. We are steadfast. We are believers. God will surely end this aggression," Mom kept assuring me.

"They can't beat Shijaiya. They just can't," my father told me.

We now live at a time in Palestine when a son lost, two kids orphaned, a young wife widowed must be compared to those who have lost ten or twenty family members at once. There is a clear attempt to ethnically cleanse Palestine, to make us leave and never come back.

## Wild rhino

Israel has been acting like a wild rhino let loose in a field of lavender. Palestinians have been acting as they should: resilient, steadfast, and even more determined.

We understand that we are not only fighting our own battle but also fighting a universal battle for justice and human rights against barbarity and occupation.

And now, like hundreds of kids who survived the horror of Israel killing either or both of their parents, Raneem and Hamza will be without a father for life. Nothing we can do will replace the warmth and the love of the father they had to lose because Israel wanted Hamas leaders to see the destruction of Gaza.

Raneem and Hamza will live to be witnesses to Israel's war on civilians. They will live and grow in an unjust world where their father can be killed because he is in his own house and the killer will not even be brought to justice because he is an Israeli soldier.

But before that happens, we will continue the struggle against Israeli ethnic cleansing of Palestinians, in the hope that before Hamza and Raneem are old enough, Israeli apartheid will be abolished forever.

*Live forever*

When my brother passed away, everyone was lamenting the death of "Mohammed." No one called him Hamada. He is again Mohammed.

But I didn't shout at them. I came to the realization that I have to finally let go and let Hamada grow into Mohammed.

Israel's barbarity to murder people in Gaza and to sever the connections between people and people, and between people and land, and between people and memories, will never succeed. I lost my brother physically, but the connection with him will remain forever and ever.

His memories, his tales, his jokes, his innocent smile will live forever through us, through his two beautiful children, and through the thousands of children who loved him on TV and in real life.

"Israel has been acting like a wild rhino let loose in a field of lavender. Palestinians have been acting as they should: resilient, steadfast, and even more determined"

—2014

# When Will Dad Come Back?

*July 2, 2015*

The last time my little niece Raneem saw her dad was when the Israeli shells were falling on the heads and houses of more than ten thousand Palestinians in Shujaiya, east of Gaza City, last summer. My brother Mohammed took the time to help guide many families to shortcuts in a desperate attempt to escape the flying shrapnel and debris.

Mohammed kept close to his wife, his baby son Hamza, and his daughter Raneem. "I will be back. Soon," he assured his weeping kids and worried wife. "I will be back. I promise."

Bringing his family and many others to a relatively safer place, he thought he should go back to help others evacuate.

My brother Mohammed never came back.

He never came back. Not because he did not keep his word, but rather because the Israeli occupation has developed a policy of destroying people and their relationships. Israel made sure my brother Mohammed and a couple of thousand Palestinians would never get to see their family members ever again.

Ever since, Raneem has been asking about her dad. "When will Dad come back? Why does Baba not come back?" she keeps asking.

Only watery eyes and pained hearts answer her quizzical looks. However we try to distract her, nothing replaces a father, let alone a loving father who made his small family his own world.

We thought that taking Raneem to see the pile of rubble that was once our house might help her understand something until my nephew, Mohammed, went to see the house with his father, my older brother.

Little Mohammed kept nagging for more than a month. He wanted nothing but to go to Shujaiya and see our house. When he was there, when he saw all the destruction and ruin, little Mohammed dangled his head and said, "I wish I had not come."

Taking Raneem and the little ones to see the pile of rubble our house was turned into is now out of the question. We are only counting on a speedy reconstruction process that will mitigate the pain and return the kids to their house.

A month after the Israeli onslaught, Raneem must have

realized that her dad would not be coming back again. She approached my mother and said, "Teta, I dislike my dad. He does not come back."

My mother has not recovered from Raneem's remark. It was like her son was killed twice. But I can only imagine the psychological damage that has already caused Raneem, who has developed a tendency toward absent-mindedness, to talk to herself.

Two months ago her mom found her giggling and mumbling. When asked what she was doing, Raneem said, "My dad gave me candy." Her tiny fist remained clenched for a long time.

*Leaving wasn't an option*

But why did so many stay behind? Why did the people of Shujaiya refuse to leave despite Israel's propaganda warning? This issue is not as simple as Zionist parrots and trolls suggest.

A Palestinian man's house is his castle. Literally. Leaving was not an option when in 2008–2009 most of the people Israel murdered were in the city center where Israel suggested they go.

Leaving was not an option because Israel wanted more than 150,000 people to leave their houses and go to the streets and schools, where Israel also targeted them.

Leaving was not an option because we still remember the 1948 ethnic cleansing massacres against the Palestinians.

Because leaving for Israel means that Palestinians never come back.

People stayed because it's their land and their houses, and because we refuse to be dictated to by an occupier and a mass murderer.

People stayed because simply finding peace and protection in one's own house is a very human act. And for that Israel sought to punish the whole Gaza Strip.

It was clear for us that Israel was tracing mobile signals and destroying houses where mobile signals emitted even if the signal came from a phone whose owner forgot it at home in the rush to escape Israeli shells.

*Grudge*

When I read the comments that Israel was planning to carpet bomb Shujaiya like it did to some areas in South Lebanon in 2006, I thought people were kidding. But it turned out Israel had this childish, though hateful, grudge against Shujaiya since the 1950s.

Shujaiya was the last area to fall under Israeli occupation in 1967. Shujaiya has always produced fighters and civil servants and defenders of human rights.

Shujaiya was a thorn in Israel's side in the first and second intifadas.

We know Salem Shamaly because his execution was caught on camera. There are many Salems in Shujaiya.

I know of at least five others, four of whom are my relatives, who were shot at close range. They were not allowed to leave their houses. Neither the Red Cross nor ambulances were allowed to evacuate them.

My distant cousin Samy Alareer tried to leave the house to seek help for his two brothers, Hassan and Abdulkarim, and his son Fathi, who were injured by the indiscriminate yet systematic shelling. On his way to fetch help, Samy was shot dead. The other three were found dead in their house with empty bullet cases all over the place.

Israeli officials were quick to brag about the death and destruction they brought upon Shujaiya. Hundreds were slain and injured, many of whom will be permanently disabled. Avichay Adraee, the Israeli army's Arabic-language spokesperson, bragged on Twitter that the Israeli army dropped 120 one-ton bombs on Shujaiya in the first two weeks of Israel's fifty-one-day attack.

Add to that the hundreds of shells and mortars with their huge error radius.

I do not have the words to do justice to the unyieldingly valiant, lion-hearted fighters of Palestine. They remained steadfast in the face of the most heinous occupation the world has known.

However, there is one thing the whole world should know: in face-to-face combat, far fewer Palestinian fighters were killed than Israeli soldiers. The heavily armed elite Israeli troops, supported with tanks, planes, and high-tech equipment, were squealing when faced with Shujaiya's modestly trained and minimally armed resistance fighters who defended their homes and families with skill and determination.

Israel's response was to arbitrarily, yet methodically, destroy houses and shell densely crowded areas. Palestinian fighters rose to the challenge of battle imposed upon them. And they fought honorably and well.

They fearlessly stood for their people.

*Betrayed by the world?*

The cost of putting up a defense in Gaza is that all Palestinians in Gaza are being punished. Israel has tightened the siege on Gaza.

Egypt has tightened its siege on Gaza.

The Palestinian Authority has tightened its siege on Gaza.

The stupidity those parties are displaying is unprecedented. Collective punishment against Palestinians has never worked. And the rules of logic say, it is foolish to do the very same things and expect different results.

But Israel, in its arrogance, the PA's Mahmoud Abbas, in his cravenness, and Arab regimes, in their complicity, seem to have agreed that a good Gaza is a starved Gaza.

With the delay of reconstruction and the clear complicity of Abbas and his cronies and the UN and its army of mercenaries living off the Palestinian plight, Raneem and

Hamza and tens of thousands will never get to go back to the house where they lived their happiest days with the most loving person they will ever know.

Raneem will have to live with the horrible memories of seeing her house become a pile of rubble.

The likes of my niece Raneem and little nephew Mohammed are purposefully being punished by Israel and the international community—first by destroying their houses and lives, and then by providing Israel with the impunity and excuses it wants, and finally by delaying the process of justice. They want these little kids to live in ruins and destruction.

Ironically, Palestinian children are expected to grow up and like Israel or see a future where peace can be achieved when the murderers of their parents and destroyers of their houses go unpunished and unaccountable.

Unless Israeli war criminals are brought to justice and the occupation ends, my fear is that these children will grow up feeling that they were betrayed by the world. We owe it to them to change that vision.

# Over the Wall

"There," points Grandma.
She had a tent that was a home.
She had a goat and a camel.
She had a rake and a fork and a trowel.
She had a machete and a watering can.
She had a grove and two hundred plants.
She had a child and another one and another one.

\*

"There," she insists.
I could not see
Because of the wall.
I could not hear
Because of the noise.
I could not smell
Because of the powder.

\*

But I can always tell,
I am sure of Grandma
Who always was
And is still
And will always be.
She smells like soil.
And smiles like soil.
And blinks like soil
When touched by rain.

\*

She has a house that is a tent
She has a key
And a memory.
She has a hope
And two hundred offspring.

\*

Grandma is here
But lives there.
"Over there!"

*May 15, 2012*

# Israel's Killer Bureaucracy

*June 28, 2016*

There are scores of ways by which Israel kills Palestinians; shedding their blood with sophisticated weapons is only one.

This is the story of my cousin Awad Alareer, who died because Israel imposes severe restrictions on Palestinian patients seeking medical treatment outside the Gaza Strip, especially in the occupied West Bank, including Jerusalem.

Awad, an eighteen-year-old from Gaza, died less than a year after he was diagnosed with bone cancer.

He needed permits to get treatment outside Gaza. Israel delayed issuing those permits on several occasions.

Awad came from a family of farmers. They were expelled from land in the greater Gaza Strip during the Nakba, the 1948 ethnic cleansing of Palestine.

Awad was named after his grandfather, who is now aged eighty-four and one of the oldest farmers in the Gaza Strip.

The elder Awad lost tens of acres when Israel was established on Palestinian lands in 1948. After 2000, he lost most of what remained of his land to the "buffer zone" that Israel imposed on Gaza.

In practice, the "buffer zone" covers everywhere in Gaza that is within two kilometers of its boundary with present-day Israel.

According to the Palestinian Center for Human Rights, approximately 30 percent of Gaza's agricultural land cannot be worked without severe personal risk. The buffer zone has caused a huge loss of livelihood.

"Awad wanted to be a farmer just like his grandfather," said his brother Basel, twenty-five. "Awad was talkative, loved by all. He was a helpful person. He even helped his mother with her chores, something young boys of his age would almost never do in Gaza."

In 2001, Israeli occupation forces opened fire at Palestinian farmers in the Shujaiya neighborhood of Gaza City, killing Awad's uncle, Tayseer Alareer, while he was farming his land. Tayseer was shot by Israeli troops at Nahal Oz, a kibbutz that also hosts a military watchtower.

The very same troops would stop occasionally at Tayseer's farm and ask for chickpeas or an ear of corn.

Little Awad grew up knowing all these things about his

family and Palestine's history. He knew that the Israeli occupation caused them poverty and pain.

He knew that the best way to resist those occupying thieves was to keep farming Palestine's land.

*Death sentence*

Last year, Awad complained of severe pain in his thigh. Painkillers did not help.

He was X-rayed at al-Shifa hospital in Gaza City.

Then he was transferred to a hospital in the Khan Younis area for an MRI scan, followed by a biopsy.

The results showed cancer.

"Cancer in Gaza is a death sentence. We do not have the proper equipment here," Awad's father, Amin Alareer, forty-seven, told me.

Egypt rarely opens Rafah—the border crossing between it and Gaza, the sole outlet for the vast majority of Gaza's approximately 1.9 million residents. "And Israel takes ages doing its so-called security vetting procedures," Amin added.

Following a short delay due to the long list of patients desperately seeking medical treatment outside Gaza, Awad's case was approved by An-Najah University Hospital in the occupied West Bank city of Nablus, inaccessible to Palestinians in Gaza without Israeli permission.

All he needed was an Israeli permit.

"Awad's file was sent to the Israeli side," said Amin. "I was supposed to accompany him. After about three weeks of waiting, both Awad and I were rejected. We had to reapply through the Palestinian Center for Human Rights."

"Awad was finally accepted," Amin added. "But I was rejected. And he had to be accompanied by someone. So we sent an application for his mother. All this while Awad's health was deteriorating."

*Urgent*

However, when Awad was ready to travel, he had already missed his appointment at An-Najah University Hospital.

So he was referred to the Augusta Victoria Hospital in East Jerusalem. Eventually, he was allowed to visit that hospital in mid-October. Tests confirmed he had bone cancer in his thigh and an operation was scheduled for December.

Awad went back to Gaza. As he waited for his operation, and for another Israeli permit to be issued, he tried to lead a normal life by going to school.

The word "normal" needs to be qualified when it comes to Gaza. His school had been bombed during Israel's 2014 attack.

Awad underwent the operation in December. Fortunately, it was a success. But Israel had hindered it by delaying the entry of a prosthesis to replace a thigh bone. That device had to be imported from Turkey. It took two weeks to arrive.

Follow-up care is of vital importance following a major operation.

It seems that the Israeli authorities know this very well. And they play dirty.

Awad stayed in Jerusalem for approximately three weeks after his operation. He then returned to Gaza.

"Awad was supposed to go back for a follow-up appointment after three weeks—on January 19 this year," his father said. "But Israel once again rejected him. Twice. And every time we had to apply from scratch as if he had never been vetted before."

It was April 5 before Awad was allowed to visit the Jerusalem hospital again. "That meant the cancer had already spread viciously to his lungs," his father said.

Awad's lung cancer was inoperable.

He was sent back to Gaza and placed in intensive care.

Three weeks later, Awad died.

*Killing the sick*

The bitter irony is that Israel markets itself as a global leader in treating various types of cancer.

"It's just too painful to know that a few miles away, Israelis who stole our land receive the best and fastest medical care," Basel, Awad's brother, told me. "If we still had our land, we could have sold some of it and sent Awad to the best hospitals in America or Europe."

Bassam al-Badri is a doctor working for a section of the Palestinian Authority in the West Bank that tries to arrange treatment for patients in Gaza. He said that if rapid action is taken, patients in Awad's situation can often be saved or at least have their lives prolonged.

"Time is a crucial element for patients with chronic diseases, especially those with tumors," he said. "A case sometimes takes twenty to thirty days for Israel to vet, when the patient cannot wait more than a few hours."

"Because Israel usually rejects applications, we end up working three or five times on the same applicant, tripling and quadrupling our effort," he added. "Each time a sick person's application is turned down, we have to start from scratch."

"We know Israel knows everything about us," he said. "Why do cases take up to a month to check? This is a deliberate attempt to kill those sick people. It's a war crime."

"International conventions guarantee medical treatment to soldiers," said Maher Shamiya, a leading official in Gaza's health ministry. "Here we're talking about kids, women, the elderly and other sick people who pose a threat to no one. And yet Israel takes forever to let them travel."

A Hamas source, who spoke on condition of anonymity, said that Israel resorts to the "deliberate arm-twisting and blackmailing of patients and their families."

Huge pressure is put on patients into giving intelligence to, "and even collaborating" with, Israel, the source added.

The Israeli authorities tell patients that they must act as informers if they are to obtain treatment outside Gaza.

This has been long documented by human rights groups and journalists.

Patients have been called to the Erez checkpoint by Israel, supposedly to receive news about their requests to travel. While at the checkpoint, the patients have been arrested.

For example, Mahmoud Abu Ful from Jabaliya refugee camp in Gaza, was detained after being summoned to Erez in April this year. He had been shot during a protest in October 2015 and had sought permission to receive treatment for his injuries in the West Bank.

The Gaza-based Al Mezan Center for Human Rights has contended that Israel is using Erez as a "trap to arrest patients, with no consideration of their health conditions."

Awad, then, is among numerous Palestinians who have been treated cruelly while they were ill. Shaking his head, my uncle reflected on the effects of that cruelty.

"Israel is a developed country," he said. "But when it comes to treating Palestinians, it's a third world country. Very, very slow. And that costs lives here."

# And We Live On . . .

And another day in Gaza

Another day in Palestine

A day in prison

And we live on

Despite Israel's very much identified flying objects

That we see more than our family and friends

And despite Israel's death sentences

Like lead

Cast upon the head

As we sleep

Like acid rain

Gnawing at our life

Clinging to it like a flea to a kitten

And stuffed in our throats

The moment we say "Amen"

To the prayers of old women and men

Despite Israel's birds of death

Hovering only two meters from our breath

From our dreams and prayers

Blocking their ways to God.

Despite that.

We dream and pray,

Clinging to life even harder

Every time a dear one's life

Is forcibly rooted up.

We live.

We live.

We do.


*May 27, 2012*

# No Justice for Gaza Youth Killed in Viral Video

*July 20, 2016*

Two years ago, during Israel's 2014 onslaught against Gaza, a young, unarmed man was killed by Israeli snipers. The killing was recorded and uploaded to YouTube and the video went viral.

The young man was Salem Shamaly. Salem, twenty-three, was helping medics and volunteers search for injured people, including what he thought might be his own family members, trapped in the rubble of their houses after an early morning bombardment by the Israeli military of the Shujaiya neighborhood of Gaza City.

Even amid the death and destruction of the 2014 onslaught, Salem's story stood out, garnering international headlines and raising questions about war crimes. But two years later, justice has not been done for Salem—or indeed any of the 2,251 Palestinians, including 551 children, Israel killed in Gaza, according to the UN's independent commission of inquiry.

To his family, Salem was a person with great potential who was plucked in his prime by a brutal occupier that refuses to let Palestinians be. The death of the family's oldest son has also precipitated decline. Salem's father, Khalil, sixty-one, has seen his small business—selling baby sanitary products—falter, and his asthma and heart conditions worsen. The family home was partially damaged during the assault and Khalil lost all his inventory, at an estimated value of some thirty thousand dollars, almost all his life savings.

## A loved boy

Salem—his name meaning safe and sound in Arabic—was born in the densely populated Shujaiya neighborhood in 1992, during the waning years of the first Palestinian intifada. He was a calm baby born on a turbulent day, his parents remember, and only cried a little. And as the first boy after six daughters and thirteen years of marriage, his was a special celebration. He would always be the oldest son, even when he eventually was just one of twelve siblings, and his father would finally be Abu Salem and have a son to take over his shop and carry on the family name.

"I always used his pet name, Salouma, until he was twenty-two. He was the apple of my eye; he was obedient. God bless his soul; he was caring and respectful," his mother Amina, forty-five, said.

And like many mothers, Amina would dote on her son.

She talked of his love of football and food, his favorite dish, *maqlouba*, and his demeanor, painting a picture of a caring and considerate child who would always ask his mother if she wanted anything before he would leave the house.

"He is loved by everyone. I was even afraid too much love would spoil him," said Umm Salem, still referring to her son in the present tense.

His father too, gave Salem special treatment. Not long after the boy could do basic maths and talk to customers, Khalil would have him help out in the shop during holidays and after school.

When Salem finished high school, he joined a local college to study accounting so that he could help with his father's business.

But when Salem's younger brother finished high school a year later and wanted to go to college, Salem decided to put his studies on hold and give his brother a chance to study at college and help him with the fees.

At the age of twenty-two, Salem had finished one year of a two-year college program and started his own business, selling children's clothing.

In one year, the young man managed to double his savings from two thousand dollars to four thousand dollars. In an economy like Gaza's, that has to constitute success. He was determined, said his mother, to start his own family and had even identified the woman he wanted to marry.

The name he only confided to his mother. And to this day, Umm Salem has not told anyone who she was.

She would never see her son married.

"Israel deprived us of Salem. And they deprived us of the children Salem would have had. And it breaks my heart," Amina said.

*A fateful day*

Most of Salem's extended family lives in Shujaiya. During Israel's assault on Gaza, the neighborhood, on the eastern part of Gaza City, was targeted with a ferocity that alarmed even US officials. John Kerry, the secretary of state, in an unguarded moment sarcastically called it a "hell of a pinpoint operation." What became known as the Shujaiya massacre, on July 20, 2014, left more than a hundred dead, more hundreds injured, and damaged or destroyed more than 1,800 homes and buildings.

Along with the nearly one hundred thousand Palestinians in the area—one of the most densely populated parts of Gaza Strip, itself of one of the most densely populated areas in the world—the Shamaly family was warned to evacuate their homes ahead of an impending assault. But some residents were stuck in their houses or went missing when the Israeli military began a ground invasion on the night of July 19.

Initial Palestinian resistance to that invasion resulted in the killing of twelve Israeli soldiers. That, in turn, elicited a wild response. For more than six hours, from the early hours of

July 20 and into the late morning, the Israeli military threw everything at the neighborhood, pummeling Shujaiya with artillery, mortars, and rockets fired from the air.

Most casualties came during that shelling. But the killings didn't end there.

At around 1:30 in the afternoon, the Israeli army announced a two-hour "humanitarian ceasefire." Salem joined a group of medics and activists heading toward Shujaiya to look for his missing relatives and other injured people.

In the video of the incident, Salem can be seen helping carry out wounded people and calling for members of his family. Then suddenly, as the volunteer who is filming is himself running over rubble, a shot rings out.

After a brief moment of confusion, during which Salem can be heard trying to make sense of the situation, another shot. In the next frame, a still alive Salem is lying down, clearly wounded. Then another shot. Then another.

According to Joe Catron, an American activist and journalist who witnessed Salem's slaying, "it should have been fairly obvious [to the snipers] that Salem was carrying nothing at all."

"The first shot missed everyone, but split our group into two. Then as Salem tried to lead his group back across the alley, three more shots struck and killed him," Catron told the Electronic Intifada.

"It was a ceasefire. And Salem was helping medics recover

injured relatives," Sameer Abu Aser, Salem's brother-in-law, told the Electronic Intifada.

Israel prevented the Red Cross from recovering the injured or the bodies of the dead, Abu Aser recounted. And for two days, Salem was missing. At that point, no one in the family knew it was Salem in the video that had by then been posted and gone viral.

His family checked with their relatives. They checked Gaza's al-Shifa hospital.

"We had to look into the faces of hundreds of people Israel had killed and injured looking for Salem. He was nowhere to be seen," Abu Aser said.

*Justice over revenge*

Abu Aser was the first to recognize Salem in the video. The toughest thing, he said, was telling his parents. They tried to venture back to Shujaiya to bring Salem back. But their relatives did not allow them. Going back was certain death.

Only after six days of waiting and hoping that Salem had managed somehow to stay alive, did they manage to retrieve his partly decomposed body.

Salem was not very political, his family say. He was always absorbed in family issues or running errands for relatives. Salem's only problem, his mother said, was that he wanted to help people.

A burning sense of injustice has taken a hold of Salem's father, Khalil. No war crimes investigation has been held into his son's death, even though the UN called his slaying an act of "willful killing."

The circumstances around his slaying, the UN's commission of inquiry concluded, "indicate that a civilian was targeted in violation of the principle of distinction. The fact that [Salem] was shot twice while lying injured on the ground is indicative of an intent to kill a protected person (either owing to his civilian status or to the fact that he was hors de combat) and constitutes an act of willful killing."

Not long after the family had retrieved Salem's body, Khalil remembered, he was asked by a Western journalist what he wanted: "Revenge, I said at the time."

Khalil paused.

"But now I am seeking justice for the blood of my son. I am seeking justice for the pain and suffering we've been through."

Khalil began counting off on his fingers.

"Israel committed many crimes, not one: they killed Salem during a ceasefire. He was unarmed and helping others. They shot him, and then shot him again when he was helpless on the ground. Soldiers did not allow medics to take him to hospital, he was left to bleed and his body was left out in the open for stray dogs and rodents to feast on."

The angry and bereaved father stopped.

"I want international organizations to sue Israel and bring the murderers to court."

# When I Stoop

*A poem for Mahmoud al-Sarsak and Lina Khattab*

The walls of my prison
Whisper to me;
They tell me stories of people who were here
Of people who lived here.
There was the weak
And there was the old.
There was the child.
There was the lady.
They were here,
But now they are there.

*

In my prison,
I talk to the walls
And they to me talk
That one day I will walk:
One day my jailer will stoop
At my feet
To unlock the chains.

It does not matter why

But he will stoop.

*

Inside my prison I draw my future

With minute details.

On the other side of the wall (Behind the bars)

Sits the jailer.

As he turns back

And looks me in the eye,

He pours mountains of boredom

And lets loose of a sigh.

I look back and smile.

He clears his throat

Blinks once then twice

And moves his lips.

I walk away

And give him my back.

I smile again Winking at the wall.

"See," it tells me

"I know," I reply,

And bend down

And shake my chains.

The look in his face,

The fear in his eyes

Both make my day.

*

Inside my prison,

I also stoop,

But when I do,

I stoop to conquer.

*July 19, 2012*

# Haunted by the Horrors of Cast Lead

*January 17, 2018, with Ahmed Abd El-Al*

The clock was approaching 11:30 in the morning. For children in Gaza, it was the last day in school before a new year holiday. The bell was due to ring shortly.

At 11:27 a.m. on December 27, 2008, Gaza was bombarded by Israeli warplanes. Instead of the anticipated school bell, the children heard the horrifying sound of bombs.

Operation Cast Lead—which began that day—was Israel's most comprehensive onslaught on Gaza in decades. Israel used its air force, navy, infantry, and artillery against a population that already had a long experience of being under military occupation and, more recently, under siege.

By the end of the offensive more than three weeks later, Israel had committed numerous massacres and used phosphoros bombs to target heavily populated areas and even shelled United Nations schools and the main UN food aid warehouse.

Israel paid $10.5 million in "compensation" for some of the damage caused. Yet it never apologized for slaughtering the innocent or targeting the UN schools that harbored hundreds of Palestinian families.

In twenty-three days, Israel killed more than 1,400 Palestinians, including more than 1,100 civilians, of whom 326 were children and 111 were women. It also injured about 5,300, some of whom remain disabled to this very day, and destroyed or damaged thousands of homes.

Yasser Ashour, now studying journalism in Istanbul, survived the attack to become an influential social media activist and a writer on Palestine. He was fourteen at the time of the offensive. There were moments when he felt life had no meaning—especially after seeing in person or on TV scores of defenseless Palestinians, including some friends, killed during Israeli strikes.

"I was preparing myself for my final exams," Ashour told the Electronic Intifada. "Then I heard massive explosions coming from everywhere. Then many other explosions followed. And it continued for twenty-three days.

Ashour believes the timing of the Israeli raids was carefully chosen, he said, "to maximize the number of casualties and terrorize Palestinians."

Ashour was part of a huge wave of schoolchildren who ran home in a situation of extreme fear.

He saw vans and lorries carrying the disfigured bodies of people killed by Israel. Today, he remains haunted by those images.

*"Butchered"*

Ashour's worst memories of that time period come from when Israel targeted his school and the surrounding area.

Located in Jabaliya refugee camp, that school—known as al-Fakhoura—was shelled by Israel on January 6, 2009. At the time, it was providing shelter to people who had to flee their homes.

Yet three days earlier, according to Judge Richard Goldstone's "Report of the United Nations Fact-Finding Mission on the Gaza Conflict," Israel had warned Palestinians "to move to central locations and attend United Nations centers."

The next day, John Ging, UNRWA director of operations in Gaza, said during a press conference: "There is nowhere safe in Gaza. Everyone here is terrorized and traumatized."

"I was one of the lucky few," Ashour said. "When we evacuated our house, we did not have to go to UN schools. My mother distributed our family among several relatives' homes, so if we were hit by Israeli missiles, some of us would get to survive."

"But I will never forget the day Israel hit my school, killing forty-four civilians," he added. "Five of them were my own classmates and friends." Defense for Children International—Palestine noted that fourteen children were killed in "close proximity" to the school. Ashour remembered shrapnel injuring people inside the school.

"The next day," he recalled, "I defied my mother's pleas and participated in the funerals. It was the least I could do. Those kids that Israel butchered were full of life and full of potential."

Although Israel claimed it targeted Hamas militants, a UN inquiry into the al-Fakhoura massacre found there was no firing from within the school and no explosives within the school.

The UN relief agency for Palestine refugees, UNRWA, "had given Israel the exact locations of all schools sheltering civilians," Ashour noted. "Israel targeted the school on purpose, to terrorize us."

Ever since the massacre, Ashour has tried to honor the memories of his classmates by exposing Israeli crimes.

"I run a few Twitter accounts with tens of thousands of followers," he said. "The battle for justice for Palestine over social media is crucial and we have to win it. We don't have Israel's billions but we have the power of truth."

### *"He never came back"*

Nirvana Modad, twenty, lost her father, uncle, and a cousin when Israeli drones targeted a funeral tent near her home in the Shujaiya neighborhood of Gaza City.

Nirvana's father wanted her to be a physician. "I always wanted to become a doctor to save lives and to fulfill my dad's dream," she said. Nirvana is studying medicine at Al Azhar University in Gaza.

Alaa Modad, her father, had just gone to the shops to buy groceries.

"My dad sent the stuff he bought home to us with my sister and went to pay his respect to a neighbor killed by Israel whose funeral tent was around the corner," Nirvana said. "And he never came back."

While Alaa was visiting it, the funeral tent was hit by two missiles fired from an Israeli drone. That was two days before the end of the offensive.

As mourners in the tent scrambled for cover, several more missiles kept coming. Nine Palestinians were killed on the spot. Many others were injured.

"To me, Israel kills my father every day," Nirvana said. "I am reminded of him by my medicine books, by my mother's hard work, by the melancholy that has overwhelmed our home ever since [his death]. And every time Israel kills a Palestinian."

Her family has continued to suffer because of Israeli state violence.

In 2014, Nirvana's cousin, Nisma Modad, lost her father during another massive Israeli offensive.

"We escaped the 2008 war by a miracle," said Nisma. "But in 2014 Israel killed my father. And God knows who Israel will kill next."

*"Sense of panic"*

Ahmed Sheikh Khalil is now aged nineteen.

As he made his way home from school on the first day of Operation Cast Lead, "I saw smoke coming from every direction of Gaza City," he said. "The explosions were shaking the ground beneath us. There was a sense of panic everywhere. I remember women running in the opposite direction, asking about their kids and telling us not to worry."

One of Khalil's cousins was killed in the attack.

"The scene of hundreds of people taking refuge in the UN school nearby haunted me for months," Khalil said. "It was like what we see on TV happening to other people or happening a long time ago."

"Like most kids in Gaza, I wanted to be a doctor," Khalil told the Electronic Intifada. "But after that war and after every assault on Gaza, I realized I could help my people in other ways."

As Khalil grew up, he became interested in media and journalism. Following another major Israeli attack on Gaza during the summer of 2014, he decided to study English.

"I want to reach and inform people from all over the world and not only Arabs or Muslims," Khalil said.

The Islamic University of Gaza, where Khalil studies English literature, had many of its laboratories destroyed by Israeli missiles in 2009.

The office of Khalil's father, who teaches history and politics at the university, was also destroyed.

"When the Israelis hit the Islamic University of Gaza, they claimed they targeted a chemical weapons lab," Khalil said.

"It was hilarious, despite the tragedy. We joked about my father's office harboring banned chemicals. But in all seriousness, it amazed me how Israel can lie and make up stories and still manage to deceive the world. I want to do something about this."

*"Too much to ask?"*

Amira al-Qirim lost her father and two siblings during Operation Cast Lead.

Amira's father, Fathi, was struck by Israeli artillery. Her brother and her sister were killed, too, during an attack on the al-Zaytoun area, south of Gaza City.

All three were left to bleed and die. No ambulance was allowed near them.

Herself injured in the attack and unable to walk, Amira crawled and hid in a neighbor's home. She was found there in a hungry and weak condition three days later.

Amira is now a stay-at-home mother of two children.

"As a kid who survived that war, and the two others that followed, I volunteered for the media to expose Israel," she said.

"I traveled to Europe for medical treatment. I spoke to people everywhere about my ordeal," Amira added.

"I sought justice by filing a complaint to the International Criminal Court at The Hague. But here we are nine years later and Israel still commits crimes every single day, and justice has not yet been done yet."

"I want my kids to live in peace," she said. "I want every kid in Palestine to grow up without the possibility that Israel will kill them, or maim them, or orphan them, or traumatize them. Is that too much to ask?"

# Mom

On Ma's face
There is a book
And life's preface.
Between these lines
And in these two caves
Life dwells.
That line is hope.
That one is love.
That death.
When she smiles,
She gives hope,
She gives love,
She gives life,
To life.

*July 30, 2012*

# "Every Palestinian Was a Target"

*April 5, 2018*

*Editor's note: On March 30, 2018, Refaat Alareer partici-*
*pated in the first day of the Great March of Return: a grass-*
*roots and overwhelmingly peaceful protest campaign along*
*Gaza's perimeter fence. Weekly demonstrations persisted*
*for months in the face of Israel's lethal repression. In this*
*spoken interview with Nora Barrows-Friedman of the*
*Electronic Intifada, Refaat recounts how the first day of*
*Gaza's Great March unfolded and assesses its significance.*
*The transcript has been edited for length and clarity.*

The day began after a couple of months, or probably close
to a month, of preparation, where people—activists—were
calling for a peaceful march in Gaza. At the beginning, it
wasn't clear how things will end up.

But on Friday, I took a taxi with my wife and my kids
and headed to the eastern parts of Gaza City, near where

my family lives, near where I used to live before Israel destroyed our house. And there were hundreds of thousands of people. The whole area was crowded. There were families, kids, elderly men, elderly women.

It seemed like everyone in Gaza City was heading toward the borders in anticipation of what's going to happen. The whole day started with people gathering, and then there was the Friday prayer. And more and more people kept coming throughout the whole day.

It was so emotional. Many people were never this close to their own villages and towns that Israel destroyed and depopulated decades ago. I saw elderly women almost weeping and shedding tears because they were so happy. They thought that they were returning back to their homes, that they were finally going to go back to the homes they left behind because Israeli militias and the Zionist gangs kicked them out by force.

Only to be met with bullets, only to be met with drones throwing tear gas canisters.

The day, in my opinion, was unprecedented in the sense that there were Palestinians belonging to all political factions. This was not a political march. It was a popular march.

Hamas did not lead this. But naturally, Hamas, Fatah, Islamic Jihad, and leftist factions were all there. People who didn't belong to any political party were also there, because everyone was calling for an end to this occupation, an end to this medieval siege imposed on Gazans here in Palestine.

Hoping for a better future, hoping for a better life.

Many people brought their food, the kids brought their toys. They tried to look their best, everyone. The mood was a festival, was cheerful.

It was like a celebration. It was like Palestine is free and people are finally returning back. This was the major theme.

Most of the slogans were focusing on the right of return, because the majority of Palestinians living in Gaza Strip are refugees. They have their own land.

I'm not a refugee myself, but my grandparents on both parts of my parents own land beyond this Israeli border imposed around Gaza. Because this is only part of Gaza; there's something called Greater Gaza. So, my father could point to areas where my grandparents would plow and plant and live for years before Israel occupied Palestine and the Gaza Strip.

The actual killing started at dawn.

There was a farmer in Hanoun who was shot and killed by Israel. In the Gaza City gathering point, near the border, even before the Friday prayer where people started gathering by hundreds and thousands, we would every now and then hear the ambulance coming and taking injured people, whether by live rounds or by tear gas.

I can't tell exactly when the shooting started in Gaza City but it started as early, as people started to gather, and even before people threw stones, or whatever they had, at the Israeli snipers shooting at Palestinians.

After the Friday prayer, I ventured closer and closer with some friends, and I realized that there were a lot more people there than we were at the back, because the whole area was crowded. One friend estimated like 100,000 or 150,000 people only in Gaza City itself.

We couldn't make calls. I wasn't sure whether this is because there were so many people crowding the area or because Israel did something. We were cut off. We didn't have internet connection. We couldn't call friends or family.

We couldn't listen to the news. So many people there were not aware of the fact that Israel was shooting and sniping Palestinian protesters.

When I came close, like three hundred meters away from the border, I saw two or three people shot, and many people suffered inhalation problems because of the tear gas. I didn't realize that many people were shot. It was later on when I went back to upload the photos and the videos I took, I heard in the news that at least seven people were killed.

I was personally stunned because the guys were far away, no stones. And I tweeted also about this. I said, not even David's sling could get the stones over the border.

So Israel, on purpose—and we've seen this in their tweets, in their Facebook, the Israeli officials were tweeting about this and were stating openly: that they will shoot at any Palestinian that approaches. And in one way or another, every Palestinian gathering there was a target.

If Israel meant to send people away by shooting them, as a matter of fact, people kept coming and coming and coming.

This is a very strong message that people were sending: that even if you're killing us, even if you're shooting us, we're not going to retreat. We're not going back. We're not going to go down. We're not going to submit. We're not going to kneel.

The march itself was peaceful. And people were insisting on this, raising their voices that we will remain here. We don't expect, of course, Israel to open the borders and to tell people to go back.

Israel has to be forced to do this. But the message was that Palestinians will keep struggling for their rights. We will keep resisting the Israeli occupation by all means available.

[These protests are] unprecedented in many ways, because Iran has just said that it's bringing people together, it's uniting people, it's reviving, sparking the hope that people have. We know that sooner or later Israel will be defeated.

But every now and then we need something to boost the morale. And nothing does this like Palestinians across the political spectrum, of all ages, of all social ranks gathering together, sitting next to each other, talking about one thing, about return, about the possibility of this march changing something.

It might not change things, not because Palestinians are losers, but because Israel is brutal.

Israel is backed by America, by the European Union, by even the Arab regimes nowadays. And Israel has never been this powerful and this arrogant. But again, this will help revive the spark, the hope that Iran has just mentioned, that Palestinians have the right to return, have everything to cling to.

And it exposes Israel as a brutal colonial power: that no matter what Palestinians do, Israel will kill them. No matter what method of resistance we will use, Israel will still brutalize us, demonize us.

Israel will be racist. Israel will be Israel. This is very clear, not just from today.

In the West Bank, we see almost on a weekly basis the peaceful, nonviolent protests in Ni'lin and Bil'in. We see how Israel brutalizes and kills and shoots the protesters. We see how Israel bans BDS activists who call for the human, the equal rights of Palestinians, and the right to return.

These Palestinians [in Gaza] were unarmed, were peacefully protesting. It's special because even the people who died—Israel tried to demonize this march because of Hamas. Yes, Israel hates Hamas. But Israel hates Palestinians.

If Palestinians shoot rockets, fire rockets, or carry guns, Israel will destroy them and will criminalize and demonize them. If Palestinians carry stones and Molotov cocktails, if Palestinians fly kites, if Palestinians breathe, Israel will hate them. And Israel will want them to be submitting and abjectly kneeling.

So the fact that some of those killed by Israel turned out to be Hamas militants, it doesn't mean that this is a military march. It doesn't mean that Hamas is behind this. It means something else.

It means that those people who belong to these military wings, those people who have guns, who are trained to shoot and maybe to snipe, chose to leave their guns behind, to be among their families and friends, to be among the unarmed peaceful protesters, to be out there again unarmed. And when these people choose this, it means something important is changing in the Palestinian community.

I'm not saying this to demonize the armed Palestinian resistance. The armed Palestinian resistance is legitimate, it's moral, it's something Palestinians have to do sometimes to defend their very existence.

But it's very significant to look at those people who are well-trained, militarily speaking, and to see them unarmed, participating, and being shot by Israel. They're trying to see what other scenarios, what other means of resistance they can be involved in.

This is not a military march. There were many people who posted videos of Israeli soldiers on the borders. If Palestinians, if some of these militants, wanted to shoot these Israeli soldiers, they were sitting ducks. But they chose not to do so.

They're trying to see if this nonviolent protest, this time, brings something new, or if the world is going to overlook the Palestinian blood, be silent, and give Israel the green light.

This is unprecedented. Not in the sense that unarmed, peaceful protests are new to Palestinians. No, Palestinians have been engaged in this kind of struggle for decades, for seven decades, even before the establishment of Israel.

But this time, everyone is coming out together.

# O'Live Tree

O, beat me more.

Hit me with your sticks;

Step on my leaves

Smother my twigs under your boots

Like how you always do.

The beating I bear;

The humiliation, I do not care

But take me not,

Steal me not.

Even if I burn,

Here I belong

And to them I shall return.

*

If you hear my talk,

You may feel my pain

But you belong not here:

You do not even know

How to touch me,

How to gently squeeze me,

How to hug me,

How to wipe off the dust,

When I am ripe,

And when I am not,

When I need water,

And when I do not,

And how to pick me

Like how they always do.

\*

Your smell and heavy boots

And the metal on your backs

And your metal bars!

For God's sakes who on earth olives picks

With metal bars for sticks?

\*

But I ramble again.

Because you won't understand

And if you understood me,

You would not, in the first place,

Be here.

*

You come and go.

I see you once or twice a year

With either flames or sticks

And I weep for the rest of the year.

But one day

My twigs shall grow,

The oil shall flow,

My people shall glow,

And you, you will go.

*October 15, 2012*

# An Introduction to Poetry

*Edited excerpt from a spoken lecture delivered to students in Advanced English Poetry at the Islamic University, Gaza*

*2021*

We all know Fadwa Tuqan, the Palestinian poet. And *please* don't introduce her as "Ibrahim Tuqan's sister." Let's talk about Fadwa Tuqan as Fadwa Tuqan.

We always fall into this trap of saying, "she was arrested for just writing poetry!" We do this a lot, even us believers in literature. "Why would Israel arrest somebody or put someone under house arrest, she only wrote a poem?"

So, we contradict ourselves sometimes. We believe in the power of literature changing lives, as a means of resistance, a means of fighting back—and then at the end of the day, we say, "She just wrote a poem!" We shouldn't be saying that.

Moshe Dayan, an Israeli general, said that, "the poems of Fadwa Tuqan were like facing twenty enemy fighters." Wow. She didn't throw stones, she didn't shoot at the invading Israeli jeeps, she just wrote poetry. And I'm falling for that again—I said she *just* wrote poetry . . .

And the same thing happened to Palestinian poet Dareen Tatour. She wrote poetry, celebrating Palestinian struggle, encouraging Palestinians to resist, not to give up, to fight back. She was put under house arrest, she was sent to prison for years.

Don't forget that Palestine was first and foremost occupied in Zionist literature and Zionist poetry. When the Zionists thought of going back to Palestine, it wasn't like, "Oh, let's go to Palestine." *(snaps fingers)*

It took them over fifty years of thinking, of planning, all the politics, money, and everything else. But literature played one of the most crucial roles here. This is our class. If I tell you, "let's move to the other class," you need guarantees that if we're going to go there we're going to find chairs, that the other place is better, is more peaceful, that we have some kind of connection, some kind of right.

So for fifty years before the occupation of Palestine and the establishment of the so-called Israel in 1948, Palestine in Zionist Jewish literature was presented to the Jewish people around the world . . . [as] "Palestine is a land without a people for a people without a land." "Palestine flows with milk and honey." "There is no one there, so let's go."

Many Jewish people were disappointed when they came to Palestine. Number one, there was no milk and honey . . . And there were people—there have *always* been people in Palestine.

So, these are examples of how poetry can be a very significant part of life.

"Don't forget that Palestine was first and foremost occupied in Zionist literature and Zionist poetry"

—2021

# My Child Asks, "Can Israel Destroy the Building If the Power Is Out?"

*May 13, 2021*

On Tuesday night, my wife, six children and I huddled in the living room of our apartment, the place least likely to take a stray hit from Israeli missiles or the debris they scatter. We were watching Al Jazeera's livestreaming of Israeli warplanes' imminent destruction of al-Jawharah (The Gem), one of Gaza's largest buildings, when the power went out.

Linah, eight years old—or, in Gazan time, two wars old—asked sheepishly if "they" could still destroy our building now that the power had gone out.

The next day, Wednesday, would be Amal's birthday. She was turning six and for the past two years has made a habit of spending six months anticipating and planning her next birthday, followed by six months reminiscing about the celebration. She is quieter than her sister Linah and still a bit naïve about the world around her. I wish she were more naïve.

When Amal woke up on Wednesday, she didn't ask for her birthday cake or candles. She knew something was wrong. She sensed the fear in the household. She heard the constant bombings.

My wife, Nusayba, insisted on celebrating anyway. "It should be a day of hope," she said. Sure, dozens of families in Gaza have lost their homes in the past few days, and scores of people have died. This is no time for celebrations or cakes. "But we cannot give in to Israel," Nusayba said.

I sneaked out of the house, making sure not to wear my Covid-19 mask, lest the Israeli drones mistake me for a target trying to hide. I bought Amal her favorite treats: Jordan almonds and chocolate biscuits. When I got back, we managed a muted rendition of "Senna Helwa" ("Happy Birthday"), far less raucously than we'd usually sing it. Amal smiled hesitantly. I looked at her and promised to take her to get the biggest cake when "this" is over.

On Monday, caught off guard by the attacks, I didn't tell my kids their bedtime stories as usual. It was a mistake that I will try not to repeat.

I've since taken to tweaking the stories because of the bombings. In the original version of one tale I've made up for the children, two kittens die of neglect because their owner is careless. Now I say the kittens belong to a little girl named Amol and they only fall sick and are nurtured back to health because Amol is good-hearted and caring.

As the habit goes in Gaza, when parents end a children's story, we offer a little rhyming refrain: "*Toota toota, khalasat el hadoota. Hilwa walla maltouta?*" ("The story is over. Was it nice or not?") The kids usually shout back, "*Maltouta!*"—meaning "not nice" and that another story is in order.

On Tuesday, when I asked the question, Linah and Amal replied nervously, in unison: "*Hilwa*." "Nice." No more.

Most Gazans I know have barely gotten any rest since the beginning of the week. As my friend Hassan Arafat tweeted: "We do not sleep; we just faint with fatigue." There are no high-tech warning systems here to alert us to incoming missiles or tell us to take shelter. We have to learn to read the patterns of Israel's wanton strikes. Being a good parent in Gaza means developing a knack for what Israel's drones and F-16s will do next.

On Wednesday night, after two hours of nonstop bombardment and Israeli missiles raining down all over the Strip—some landing just a few hundred meters away from our building—we finally managed to catch some sleep. The missiles shake the whole area for several seconds. Then you hear screams. Shouting. More screams. Whole families turn out onto the street. Our kids were all sat up in bed, shaking, saying nothing.

Then comes the intolerable indecision: I am caught between wanting to take the family outside, despite the missiles, shrapnel and falling debris, and staying at home, like sitting ducks for the American-made, Israeli-piloted planes. We stayed at home. At least we would die together, I thought.

The deafening strikes destroy Gaza's infrastructure, cutting off roads leading to hospitals and water supplies, bringing down access to the internet. Many of the targets Israel hits have no strategic value. Israel knows this, and knows how it unnerves us. I wonder what those officers do in their command centers: Do they draw straws on which block to annihilate? Do they roll a dice?

Wednesday was the last day of Ramadan. The holy month of fasting ends with Eid al-Fitr, a celebration considered to be the second-happiest in Islam. Children traditionally wear new clothes and receive cash gifts and toys from relatives. Muslims in Palestine visit their families and eat together. Not this Eid, though.

By early Thursday, sixty-nine people in Gaza were reported to have been killed in Israel's airstrikes, including commanders of Hamas, the group that governs the Strip, and seventeen children. At least seven Israelis, including one child, had died from the hundreds of rockets fired by Hamas.

In 2014, during the last war, Israel killed my brother Hamada; it destroyed my apartment when it brought down the family home that housed forty people. It killed my wife's grandfather, her brother, her sister and her sister's three kids. We have not overcome that trauma yet. We have not finished rebuilding the homes Israel obliterated then.

Nusayba and I are a perfectly average Palestinian couple: Between us we have lost more than thirty relatives.

These days, as we lie in the darkness at night, I fear the worst—and I fear the best. If we come out of this alive, how will my children's psyches fare in the years to come, living in constant dread of the next attack?

On Tuesday, Linah asked her question again after my wife and I didn't answer it the first time: Can they destroy our building if the power is out? I wanted to say: "Yes, little Linah, Israel can still destroy the beautiful al-Jawharah building, or any of our buildings, even in the darkness. Each of our homes is full of tales and stories that must be told. Our homes annoy the Israeli war machine, mock it, haunt it, even in the darkness. It can't abide their existence. And, with American tax dollars and international immunity, Israel presumably will go on destroying our buildings until there is nothing left."

But I can't tell Linah any of this. So I lie: "No, sweetie. They can't see us in the dark."

# I Am You

Two steps: one, two.

Look in the mirror:

The horror, the horror!

The butt of your M-16 on my cheekbone

The yellow patch it left

The bullet-shaped scar expanding

Like a swastika,

Snaking across my face,

The heartache flowing

Out of my eyes dripping

Out of my nostrils piercing

My ears flooding

The place.

Like it did to you

70 years ago

Or so.

\*

I am just you.

I am your past haunting

Your present and your future.

strive like you did.

I fight like you did.

I resist like you resisted

And for a moment,

I'd take your tenacity

As a model,

Were you not holding

The barrel of the gun

Between my bleeding

Eyes.

*

One. Two.

The very same gun

The very same bullet

That had killed your Mom

And killed your Dad

Is being used,

Against me,

By you.

*

Mark this bullet and mark in your gun.

If you sniff it, it has your and my blood.

It has my present and your past.

It has my present.

It has your future.

That's why we are twins,
Same life track
Same weapon
Same suffering
Same facial expressions drawn
On the face of the killer,
Same everything
Except that in your case
The victim has evolved, backward,
Into a victimizer.
I tell you.
I am you.
Except that I am not the you of now.

*

I do not hate you.
I want to help you stop hating
And killing me.
I tell you:
The noise of your machine gun
Renders you deaf
The smell of the powder
Beats that of my blood.

The sparks disfigure

My facial expressions.

Would you stop shooting?

For a moment?

Would you?

*

All you have to do

Is close your eyes

(Seeing these days

Blinds our hearts.)

Close your eyes, tightly

So that you can see

In your mind's eye.

Then look into the mirror.

One. Two.

I am you.

I am your past.

And killing me,

You kill you.

*November 1, 2012*

# Gaza Asks: When Shall This Pass?

*2022*

In 1985, when I was a first grader, I was awakened by a hustle and bustle of noise downstairs. It was pitch-dark. I could hear my mom sobbing. There were women comforting her. I had never heard Mom weep before. It still haunts me to this day.

When I snuck downstairs to see what was going on, I found that my dad's old mahogany Peugeot 404 had its front and rear windshields shattered, the passenger door was wide open, and blood was all over the place. (Does this explain my fear of riding "shotgun" when we drive our car?)

My father had been coming back home that night from work and it was his business partner's turn to drive. As they passed the Nahal Oz military crossing from Israel into the Gaza Strip, out of nowhere, a hail of bullets struck their car. It was in the midst of that chatter that I first heard the words "the army," "Israel," "the Jews," and "shooting." I almost never bought a toy gun as a kid.

Did the sleepy soldier's finger slip and pull the trigger? We did not know. Did he shoot the car for fun? We did not know. There was no investigation. And no one was held accountable.

My father was injured in the attack and had to deal with the shrapnel of the bullet that ricocheted and hit his shoulder. For decades, especially in cold weather, he suffered from some sort of phantom pain. The whole family had to live with the trauma that our father and breadwinner was almost killed in an instant, a trauma in whose shadow we still live. I still go to check on my family members every time I hear bullets outside. Every time I am made to recall those memories, I remember the women's comforting words in my home: "It shall pass."

Scorched childhood. Traumatic memories. Pain. Loss. And there is more.

*Cheshire-ish smiles*

Four years later, I was minding my own business (only being a nuisance to one of my classmates) in the schoolyard, when a sizable rock whizzed and hit me in the head. I recall that I blacked out for some time. Bleeding profusely, I pressed my left hand on my head to stop the bleeding. The little kids swarmed around me, all pointing up to the adjacent four-story house whose roof was occupied by Israeli soldiers for a military post.

The Israeli soldier who threw the rock was smiling from ear to ear, a smile reminiscent of the Cheshire Cat from *Alice in Wonderland*. The doctor who dressed the wound kept comforting me, "It's nothing. It shall pass."

Just two years later, I encountered another soldier who grinned like that from ear to ear. He shot me with a hail of rubber-coated bullets straight in the chest and arm as I hurled stones at the military jeeps invading the Shujaiya neighborhood.

"It shall pass," my grandmother told me as she poured cold water on my arm and chest, promising never to tell my father I got shot, but never telling me off for being one of the intifada's (uprising's) stone throwers.

Early in my life, I learned one main thing about the Israeli occupation: the best course of action, whether or not you throw stones, is to run when you see soldiers, because who they target is largely arbitrary. Even if you go about your life in a peaceful way, minding your own business, if soldiers catch you, they will beat you up, or worse, arrest you. This is why Israel has killed a lot more civilians than freedom fighters.

I have never been caught in my life. I was shot three times with rubber-coated metal bullets and was beaten only when the soldiers stormed our home. They slapped me, my brothers, and cousins dozens of times because when they checked, our hearts were racing, a sign we were running and possibly throwing stones. We were between eight and eleven years old then. Our hearts always raced.

As I grew into a proud stone thrower at the age of twelve, the thing I feared most was my dad's wrath. He worked in Israel as a laborer and, if he had caught me throwing stones, he would have rebuked me. My dad was not heartless or abusive. He just knew that if the Israeli forces had caught me, he would have lost his work permit. I survived the first intifada (1987–1993), in which Israel killed over 1,600 Palestinians and injured thousands. I was lucky I escaped Israel's bullets and Yitzhak Rabin's "broken bones" policy.

That was not true of my friend Lewa Bakroun, then thirteen, who was chased by an Israeli settler who shot him dead from point-blank range in front of his classmates. The Israeli settler did not want to punish Lewa for throwing stones, for Lewa did not throw stones. The settler wanted to teach those who threw stones a lesson, by killing a kid. In front of the eyes of scores of little scared kids going back home from school. And a few meters away from Lewa's home. His mother's shrieks still ring in my ears.

In the midst of writing this, I called my childhood friend and Lewa's soulmate and cousin, Fady, to check the date of Lewa's murder. Fady was at Shifa Hospital. He informed me that Haniya, Lewa's mother, had a cancerous tumor and couldn't travel for treatment because of the Israeli siege on Gaza.

"It shall pass," I comforted Fady.

"It shall pass," he echoed nonchalantly.

## The second intifada

In 1997, as an undergraduate, I chose to major in English literature. I had many stories to tell in English to wider audiences. As the second intifada raged and as Israel started massacring Palestinians again, I began to learn more about Palestine and the military occupation. I wanted to do more with my English skills and my experience being born and raised under Israeli occupation. I remember when I first heard the question, "How many more Palestinians should be massacred for the world to care about our lives?" I thought, naïvely, that repeating the question would change people. It would make them think and reconsider their positions. I posted it all over the forums I was part of then. But Israel kept killing us. And Israel kept destroying our lives. And boy was I wrong about the world's reaction!

In 2001, Israeli occupation forces opened fire on Palestinian farmers in the Shujaiya neighborhood in Gaza City, killing a distant cousin, Tayseer Alareer, while he was farming his land. Tayseer was shot by Israeli troops at Nahal Oz, a kibbutz that also hosted a military watchtower. This was the very same military post where my father was shot about twenty-five years earlier.

Tayseer was a farmer. He was not a fighter. He was not a stone thrower. He was as simple as a farmer minding his own business can be. But that did not shield him from Israeli fire. Ironically, Israeli troops would occasionally stop at Tayseer's farm and ask for chickpeas or an ear of corn. Was the soldier who killed Tayseer one of those who enjoyed the occasional free chickpeas or corn? We did not know. Because Tayseer's life did not matter, and therefore there was no investigation into the shooting.

Tayseer left behind three little kids, a distraught widow, and a farm without a farmer. At the funeral, people comforted the unknowing kids. Everyone insisted: It shall pass. It shall pass.

As the second intifada escalated, Israel slaughtered more and more Palestinians, some of whom were relatives, friends, and neighbors.

*Stories of Gaza*

After Israel's Operation Cast Lead (2008–2009), which claimed the lives of over 1,400 Palestinians in twenty-three days, life in Gaza was unbearable. Israel tightened its noose around Gaza's neck. Israel literally counted the calories entering Gaza. The plan was to keep Palestinians hungry but not starve them to death. Mail, books, timber, chocolate, and most raw materials were all banned. The war made tens of thousands homeless.

I was a young academic with a master's degree in comparative literature from University College London, teaching world literature and creative writing at the Islamic University in Gaza (IUG). I remember, during the onslaught, spending the twenty-three days telling my little kids, Shymaa, Omar, and Ahmed, many stories to distract them. Some were stories my mother told me as a child or variations on her stories, featuring my children as the heroes and saviors every now and then. Even though bombs and missiles could be heard in the background, my children were transfixed, listening to my stories like never before. I spent most of the time trying to make sure I held these storytelling sessions in the room least likely to take a hit from stray Israeli missiles. As a Palestinian, I have been brought up on stories and storytelling. It's both selfish and treacherous to keep a story to yourself—stories are meant to be told and retold. If I kept a story to myself, I would be betraying my legacy, my mother, my grandmother, and my homeland.

My stories were both an end and a means. As I told stories to my children to distract, soothe, and educate them, I felt very close to my mother and to my grandparents. The stories were my window to my mother's past, to my past, as I started reliving every minute she had spent in a homemade panic room her grandfather had prepared for them before Israel first invaded Gaza decades ago. And I remembered how my heart would skip a beat each time she told us of the many near-death experiences she and her family had to endure. The mere idea of my mother coming very close to death, just for being, still transfixes me.

One day, Mom told us she had been on her way to school when a shell exploded a few meters away from her. She kept walking and attended her classes. The following day she woke up and went to school like nothing had happened the day before, like she was rejecting the rule of the shells. (In retrospect, I believe that's why I almost never skipped a class in my life.) But my mother has outlived Israel's brutal invasion, and so have her stories. During the 2008–2009 attacks on Gaza, the more bombs Israel detonated, the more stories I told. When bombs interrupted the stories, I calmed my little ones down: "It shall pass," I lied.

Telling stories was my way of resisting. It was all I could do. And it was then that I decided that if I lived, I would dedicate much of my life to telling the stories of Palestine, empowering Palestinian narratives, and nurturing younger voices.

Gaza went back to normal, as we dusted ourselves off from the most immediate pain and agony that came with the Israeli attacks of "Cast Lead." Only this time there were new piles of bodies, houses, orphans, ruins, and stories to tell. I went back to my classrooms and to my students at the English Department of IUG, whose newest, highly equipped laboratory building had been bombed by Israel. Scars were everywhere. Every single person in Gaza had to mourn a loved one. I started inviting my friends and students to write about what they had to endure and to bear witness to the anguish Israel had caused.

Writing is a testimony, a memory that outlives any human experience, and an obligation to communicate with ourselves and the world. We lived for a reason, to tell the tales of loss, of survival, and of hope," I told my students. And this is how *Gaza Writes Back* was born. I started assigning my students and training them to write short stories based on the realities they and their families and friends experienced. *Gaza Writes Back* is a book of short stories written in English by young Palestinians from Gaza, published in the United States in 2014. It includes twenty-three stories to correspond to the twenty-three days of Israeli terror in 2008 and 2009. The book is now available in seven languages. During our tour in the US and around the world, where we spoke at many events about the book, the solidarity, support, and activism felt tangible. We felt so good when people listened and sympathized and expressed their support.

And I believed that *Gaza Writes Back* would make a difference. It might help shift public opinion. It might help alleviate the pain and suffering that Palestinians in Gaza, the West Bank, and Jerusalem and everywhere experienced as part of their lives. But can a story or a poem change the mind or the heart of the occupiers? Can a book make a difference? Will this calamity, this occupation, this apartheid pass? It seems it won't. A few months later, in July 2014, Israel waged its most barbaric campaign of terror and destruction in decades, killing over 2,400 Palestinians and destroying over twenty thousand homes in fifty-one days.

*2014 war*

During the 2014 war, Israel bombed the administration building of IUG. The missiles destroyed the English Department offices, including my office where I stocked so many stories, assignments, and exam papers for potential book projects.

When I started teaching at IUG, I met young students, most of whom have never been outside Gaza and have suffered greatly under Israeli occupation. This suffering became even worse when Israel tightened its siege in 2006. Many of them could not go to the West Bank for family visits, or to Jerusalem for a simple religious ritual, or to the United States or the United Kingdom for research and visits. Books, along with thousands of other commodities, were not normally allowed into Gaza. The consequences of putting this young generation in the dark, the world must know, has far worse ramifications than we would ever expect.

At the beginning, my students must have found it difficult to study Yehuda Amichai (because he is an Israeli Jew!) or to accept my "progressive" views about Shakespeare's Shylock or Dickens's Fagin. For many, Fagin was the source of evil; the embodiment of the devil that destroys society by murdering, at least metaphorically, its future, and the little ones, by turning them into thieves and murderers.

Only later were my students able to see that Fagin was a mere product of a society that hates those who are different, those with a darker skin or a different race or having different stories. They came to realize Fagin was even better than the church itself. They saw him offering a shelter for the homeless and making the likes of Oliver feel happy and hopeful for a little bit. Fagin, the Jew, was no longer a Jew. He was a human being, just like any one of us. Fagin's refusal to wake Oliver up to send him to break into some house—commenting, "Not now. Tomorrow. Tomorrow"—was no longer seen as ironic, but as evidence of a man with a heart. The most challenging question I asked was, "What would you do if you were Fagin?"—a question that invited my students to reconsider issues of race and religion, and transcend them to embrace much higher concepts of humanity and shared interests.

But teaching Shakespeare's *The Merchant of Venice* was trickier. To many of my students Shylock was beyond repair. Even Shylock's daughter hated him! However, with the open-mindedness, commitment to dialogue, and respect for all cultures and religions that IUG promotes, I worked very closely with my students to overcome all prejudices when judging people, or at least when analyzing literary texts.

Shylock, therefore, also evolved from a simplistic idea of a Jew who wanted a pound of flesh just to satisfy some cannibalistic primitive desires of revenge into a totally different human being. Shylock was just like us Palestinians, exposed constantly not only to Israeli aggression and destruction and racism, but to Israel's war machine of misinformation and defamation. Shylock had to endure many religious and spiritual walls erected by an apartheid-like society. Shylock was in a position where he had to choose between total submission and humiliation, relegated to living as a subhuman, and resisting oppression by the means available to him. He chose to resist, just like Palestinians do nowadays.

Shylock's "Hath not a Jew eyes?" speech was no longer a pathetic attempt to justify murder, but rather an internalization of long years of pain and injustices. I was not at all surprised when one of my students found the similarities between us and Shylock so striking that she altered the speech to:

Hath not a Palestinian eyes? Hath not a Palestinian hands, organs,

dimensions, senses, affections, passions; fed with

the same food, hurt with the same weapons,

subject to the same diseases, heal'd by the same means,

warm'd and cool'd by the same winter and summer

as a Christian or a Jew is? If you prick us, do we not bleed?

If you tickle us, do we not laugh? If you poison us,

do we not die? And if you wrong us, shall we not revenge?

Perhaps the most emotional moment in my six-year teaching career in IUG's English Department was when I asked my students which character they identified with more: Othello, with his Arab origins, or Shylock the Jew. Most students felt they were closer to Shylock and more sympathetic to him than to Othello. Only then did I realize that I had managed to help my students grow and shatter the prejudices they had grown up with because of the occupation and the siege. Sadly, the exam papers which I stored in my office were set ablaze in a way that echoes how Shylock was stripped of his money and possessions. I always wanted to make use of the answers and compile them into a book.

## A merry sport

Soon after Israel destroyed the administration building, an Israeli army spokesman declared on Twitter that they destroyed a "weapons development center" at the Islamic University. However, a few hours later, Israel's defense minister issued a press release giving a different reason why Israel bombed IUG: "IUG was developing chemicals, to be used against us." Of course, there was no shred of evidence for this claim. We just have to take it for granted that Israel never ever lies. We are even supposed to ignore the glaring inconsistency in how the pretext was upgraded from a mere center to develop weapons to one that develops "chemicals."

My talks about tolerance and understanding, Boycott, Divestment, and Sanctions (BDS) and nonviolent resistance, and poetry and stories and literature did not help us or protect us against death and destruction. My motto "This too shall pass" became a joke to many. My mantra "A poem is mightier than a gun" was mocked. With my own office gone by wanton Israeli destruction, students would not stop joking about me developing PMDs, "Poems of Mass Destruction," or TMDs, "Theories of Mass Destruction." Students joked that they wanted to be taught chemical poetry alongside allegorical and narrative poetry. They asked for short-range stories and long-range stories instead of normal terms like short stories and novels. And I was asked if my exams would have questions capable of carrying chemical warheads!

But why would Israel bomb a university? Some say Israel attacked IUG just to punish its twenty thousand students or to push Palestinians to despair. While that is true, to me IUG's only danger to the Israeli occupation and its apartheid regime is that it is the most important place in Gaza to develop students' minds as indestructible weapons. Knowledge is Israel's worst enemy. Awareness is Israel's most hated and feared foe. That's why Israel bombs a university: it wants to kill openness and determination to refuse living under injustice and racism. But again, why does Israel bomb a school? Or a hospital? Or a mosque? Or a twenty-story building? Could it be, as Shylock put it, "a merry sport"?

*Personal loss*

In my *New York Times* piece titled "My Child Asks: Can Israel Destroy Our Building If the Power Is Out?" printed on May 13, 2021, I wrote that my wife, Nusayba, and I are a perfectly normal Palestinian couple—we have over thirty relatives killed by Israel in the past two decades.

One of Israel's most heinous onslaughts against Gaza in 2014 was the massacre of Shujaiya, a neighborhood adjacent to the border with Israel east of Gaza City. Shujaiya is one of the most populated areas in the world with over one hundred thousand people, mostly children, living on a very small patch of land. During the massacre, Israel bombarded the area for ten hours, nonstop. At dawn, the shelling stopped, giving people a bit of time to run for their lives—only for the shelling to resume. The images of the elderly, women, children, and young people dead in the streets and in the safety of their homes still haunt us all.

Among the people Israel murdered in 2014 was my brother Mohammed. Israel widowed his wife and orphaned his two kids, Raneem and Hamza. Israel also killed four members of my extended family. Our family home was destroyed, and so were the homes of my uncles and relatives. Nusayba lost her brother, grandfather, and cousin. But the most horrific massacre happened when Israel targeted my wife's sister's home. Israel killed Nusayba's sister, three of her sister's kids, and her sister's husband, leaving Amal and Abood injured and orphaned. The rest of the family members were injured and had to be dug out from under the rubble. Nusayba's father's home and her brothers' homes were destroyed, too.

The wounds Israel inflicted in the hearts of Palestinians are not irreparable. We have no choice but to recover, stand up again, and continue the struggle. Submitting to the occupation is a betrayal to humanity and to all struggles around the world.

At the end of the day, nothing Palestinians or those who support Palestine do will please Israel or the Zionist lobby. And Israeli aggression will continue unabated. BDS. Armed struggle. Peace talks. Protests. Tweets. Social media. Poetry. All are terror in Israel's books. Even Archbishop Desmond Tutu, hailed by most people as a champion of justice not only against apartheid South Africa but racial segregation everywhere, especially in Palestine, was slandered as a bigot and an antisemite. Renowned actor Emma Watson was attacked and accused of antisemitism for daring to post in support of Palestine solidarity on Instagram. It is not surprising then that Refaat Alareer or Ali Abunimah or Steven Salaita or susan abulhawa or Mohammed or Muna El-Kurd or Remi Kanazi is constantly attacked by Zionist trolls who wrongly use the antisemitism slander against us. No matter how mild the criticism of Israel's crimes or how slight the support for Palestinian rights, the Zionist lobby will attempt to scorch the earth to prevent that. This is further evidence that Israel is not merely after Palestinian armed resistance, but it is also after the very existence of Palestinians.

I know that many Palestinians ask if more can be done, if free people can do more to prevent Israel from continuing to commit horrifying crimes against us. Can popular resistance, or armed struggle, or BDS, or pro-Palestine groups like Jewish Voice for Peace, or Black Lives Matter activists or indigenous struggle activists, do more to exert pressure and prevent further Israeli aggressions, to bring those Israeli war criminals to justice and to end their impunity? When will this pass? When will it be enough? How many dead Palestinians are enough? How many massacres are enough?

I recoil in horror and shudder as I write this—I am exposed, naked, and vulnerable. Reliving the horrors Israel brought on us is one thing, but disclosing your life and your most intimate moments of fear and terror, where you spill your heart out, is another. Sometimes late at night when insomnia hits, I wonder if it is all worth it, if anything will ever change.

When I was approached to write for this book, the promise was that it will effect change and that policies, especially in the United States, will be improved. But, honestly, will they? Does a single Palestinian life matter? Does it?

Reader, as you peruse these chapters, what can or will you do, knowing that what you do can save lives and can change the course of history? Reader, will you make this matter?

Gaza is not and should not be a priority only when Israel is shedding Palestinian blood en masse. Gaza, as the epitome of the Palestinian Nakba, is suffocating and being butchered right in front of our eyes and often live on TV or on social media.

It shall pass, I keep hoping. It shall pass, I keep saying. Sometimes I mean it. Sometimes I don't. And as Gaza keeps gasping for life, we struggle for it to pass, we have no choice but to fight back and to tell her stories. For Palestine.

# Freshly Baked Souls

As fire balls and sparks descend,

And the little ones rejoice,

Look up, and cheer, unable to comprehend,

Sooner than they expect

They will be blown

(It's none of their wishes

If only they had known!)

And more freshly grilled balls of flesh ascend.

And fall on full dishes

And fill the boxes.

And the hollow minds.

The full bellies.

They look down. Rejoice. Cheer.

"Freshly baked!"

"Freshly baked!"

"Who wants freshly baked flesh for breakfast?"

"Throw me a piece."

"Throw me four.

I have just eaten but crave for more."

*

The hearts are not hearts.
The eyes can't see
There are no eyes there
The bellies craving for more
A house destroyed except for the door
The family, all of them, gone
Save a photo album
That has to be buried with them
No one was left to cherish the memories
No one.
Except freshly baked souls in bellies.
Except for a poem.

*November 20, 2012*

# Without Consequences, Israel Will Continue to Murder Palestinians

*August 7, 2022*

Amal is now two wars old.

No one ever gets used to being bombarded every year or so. The kids in particular live in constant fear. But it does become part of life.

As the Israeli missiles rained down on Gaza City on Friday, my daughter Amal, six, asked her mom, memories of last year's horror still fresh: "Will there be another war?"

During the assault, my children, especially Linah, nine, and Amal, have been mostly quiet. Amal has tried to sleep and Linah lay down in the living room. At night, like most kids in Gaza, they shriek in fear each time they hear an explosion. A report published by EuroMed found that about 91 percent of Palestinian children live in constant trauma and terror due to recurrent Israeli attacks.

Nothing can prepare you for this. Israel has been bombarding Gaza ever since the second intifada. We never get used to the bombs. And we never know how to deal with the sheer terror and absolute Israeli savagery. No lies or hugs or sweets can calm the kids down. When the bombs fall, the kids will always shriek in utter fear. The lies that things will be alright and that these are fireworks no longer work.

By Sunday morning, Israel had killed at least thirty Palestinians, including two Islamic Jihad leaders, and a little girl, Alaa Qaddum, five.

Well over 250 Palestinians have been injured and several homes and buildings have been destroyed or damaged.

As I was writing this on Saturday morning, Israel had just struck a wedding in the northern Gaza Strip, reportedly killing the groom's mother.

*Flimsy and murderous*

Israel's pretext this time is as flimsy as can be. After detaining a senior Islamic Jihad leader in the occupied West Bank, Israel said it was engaged in a "preemptive operation" to stop alleged missile attacks before they start.

This is like Israel's war on Gaza in May 2021 and its massive 2014 attack and the many escalations between them. And it brings back memories of Israel's bombing campaigns in 2012, 2008–2009, 2006, and many others, several of which coincided with Israeli elections.

Palestinian resistance fighters, as expected, reacted eventually by firing volleys of homemade missiles at Israeli military targets. By doing so, they are affirming the Palestinian right to self-defense and liberation.

Many Palestinians have seen countless of their loved ones murdered in their sleep, or when they were resting and generally minding their own business. If Israel will kill us regardless of who we are or what we are doing, then, many Palestinians believe, why not die fighting and defending our very existence?

There is no one more determined or dangerous than a person who has nothing to lose.

During the May 2021 aggression, according to Airwars, in more than 70 percent of Israeli attacks that killed Palestinian civilians, there were no reports of any casualties from the resistance. In other words, civilians were the only victims.

According to B'Tselem, an Israeli rights group, nearly two-thirds of the more than 2,200 Palestinians Israel killed in Gaza in 2014 were civilians.

Notice that such statistics usually count Palestinian civilian police or resistance fighters killed in their homes as they slept as militants.

Given these realities, I am certain that civilians, mainly children, women, and the elderly, are not collateral damage—rather they are Israel's main targets.

*Sweets and guilt*

But despite all that, I want to make things seem okay to my children. I can't prevent their eyes from seeing what they see, or their ears from hearing the bombs. I cannot protect their hearts from the Israeli mayhem.

So, I go out to buy sweets. But to venture out is to put yourself in grave peril. One might get killed simply being in the street, not that remaining at home is much safer.

I don't take the elevator if the power is on. Not that the stairs are safer.

I make sure not to walk near buildings or under trees lest I should appear suspicious to Israeli drones. Not that walking in the middle of the street is any safer.

And then there is the guilt. The guilt of being able to go out while hundreds of thousands can't. The guilt of being able to buy bread and other essentials while hundreds of thousands cannot afford such necessities.

Taking my time to double check I am not buying Israeli products, I get several things: cookies, chips, chocolate pudding and sweets. When I come back home, Amal does not rush to greet me as she usually does. She does not rush to ransack the bags to snatch and devour her favorite sweets. She remains motionless, almost lifeless.

Israel has the "right to defend itself," says the American administration. So, too, say British and European statements.

Several officials, including from the UN and the International Committee of the Red Cross, waited for hours for the Palestinian resistance to react to issue tame condemnations calling on "all sides to avoid further escalation."

The UN's Tor Wennesland announced he was "[d]eeply concerned by the ongoing escalation between #Palestinian militants & #Israel" . . . of course only after the Palestinian resistance struck back with what little they have.

These vicious lies of Israel defending itself attempt to create a false moral equivalence that both sides are to blame. This obscures rather than reveals.

It is really not hard to understand why this keeps happening, why my youngest daughter is two wars old already. Israeli immunity from criticism and consequences along with the political and financial support it unconditionally receives from the West (and even from Arab countries) are the reasons it feels safe to continue to murder Palestinians.

*Lives and votes*

Indeed, we understand that when Israel escalates against us, its political leaders not only receive more votes in elections, they receive more support from Western countries.

With Israeli polls projecting Benjamin Netanyahu to win a majority of sixty-plus seats in upcoming elections, the current interim coalition government, considered to be "moderate" by many liberals in the West, must have thought a quick war on Gaza might appeal to Israel's electorate.

Palestinians have become accustomed to Israel's carnage when elections approach. Israeli leaders know the best way to win votes is to flex their muscles. Our problem, in other words, is not with Netanyahu or the Likud but with the Israeli occupation itself.

Yet it is wrong to assume Israel kills Palestinians only when there are elections on the horizon. Israeli and Zionist militias have been massacring Palestinians for approximately a hundred years now. Israel is not satisfied with anything but total victory for its colonial rule.

Palestinians are not Ukrainians for the world to care about. It's not Russia bombing us for the world to send us sophisticated weapons to defend ourselves. We are not mostly blond with blue eyes. We are not Jews. And for being the wrong sort of people, it seems, we have to starve, to live in fear and terror, and die without anyone lifting a finger.

*Lies and questions*

The sweets and the kids' favorite pudding remain untouched. Linah and Amal cower against the walls of the living room. They refuse to eat or be entertained. Nusayba, my wife, tells them yet another set of little lies: the bombings are far away, the missiles are "ours," and this too shall pass.

There will be more Israeli wars and more Israeli massacres. Will Israeli war criminals ever pay for their crimes? Will Arab countries rushing to normalize ties with Israel see it for what it is: an entity built on the violent dispossession and dislocation of Palestinians? Can grassroots organizations and free people wherever they may be, put more pressure on their governments to boycott and hold Israel accountable?

If not, the lies, little and big, will continue. Israel will continue to shed Palestinian blood, for fun or for political gain, or to consolidate its occupation.

Or simply because it can.

# To Our Friend in Letters
## Dareen Tatour

To do or not to do
I mutter a line of verse or two
And I am in prison.
I am in prison for writing poetry.

I am in prison
For muttering poetry
For daring to think
For trying to pull a Shakespeare
I am in prison
Words . . . words . . . words . . . words . . .
And I am in prison
For words.

What would Hamlet say?
Chains to the sweet?
Cruel to be cruel?
To die to die?
No chance to dream?

\*

I am at the stake
I am being burnt
For being here
For writing poetry
I am in prison.

\*

To those in prison
For daring to think
For daring to write
For daring
For being
For breathing
Sweets to the sweet.

I am free.
There is nothing bad about poetry
But Israel makes it so.
So, resist, my people, resist them.
Resist, my people, resist them.

\*

Everything is rotten in Israel.

It is rotten to the core.

Its letters:

The "I" is not an eye;

They do not see here.

The "S" snakes into my prison.

Ra

Eel.

Yuck!

Look who is in prison now!


israel.


*October 2, 2018*

# Raising Children Under Israel's Bombs

*September 8, 2022*

*Editor's note: Between August 5 and August 7, 2022, Israel killed more than thirty people in Gaza. In subsequent weeks, Israeli forces conducted widespread arrest campaigns in the West Bank, where they also raided the offices of seven Palestinian human rights groups. In the following excerpts from a spoken interview conducted for the Electronic Intifada podcast by Nora Barrows-Friedman, Refaat Alareer discusses the strains of being a parent under Israeli assault, the motives driving Israeli offensives, and the impact of Israel's economic blockade of Gaza, which was imposed in 1991 and tightened after 2006. The transcript has been edited for length and clarity.*

Israel is doing non-stop campaigns of "mowing the lawn," killing Palestinians and putting us in our place, in a corner where we can't do anything to defend ourselves and our rights.

When Israel started bombing, my little Amal asked her mother if there is going to be another war. It was really hard on me as a father, as a parent: a little kid, five or six years old, preparing in three weeks to start school, and she's asking about another war happening in her short life. This is what the kids in Gaza go through every year, every two years maximum.

And in between these huge, massive campaigns, Israel also never stops bombing Palestinians. It's very traumatic. It's like a nightmare that you never wake from. A nightmare that leads to a nightmare that leads to a nightmare, like a Pandora's box.

As a father, as a parent, we are helpless. We don't know what to do. We can't find a solution for this.

There is no normal in Gaza. We never have normal days because even when we go back [after a war], we go back to the siege, the occupation, to dying slowly, to lacking electricity, lacking power, lacking even sometimes basics for food, books, school materials, clothes; with Israel sometimes tightening the noose and closing the border, not allowing Palestinian cancer patients and others to go to seek treatment.

The aftermath [of an Israeli offensive in Gaza] is usually no bombs but a lot of talks about what happened and how things happened. You are always forced to listen to the little ones talking about the bombs, and what happened, and who was afraid, who wasn't afraid. You know, some-times kids try to prove that they were heroes despite what happens during the bombing.

Usually there are screams, there are tears, you know, you can imagine how kids react when there is a bomb nearby. In the aftermath, it's usually kids talking about wars, sometimes like politicians speaking about the missiles and the bombings. Or it would usually be very devastating when they realize that a friend of theirs was killed, or a little one that went to nursery with them was killed, or that the family house of relatives was destroyed, like what happened to my relatives last year.

My in-laws' house was destroyed, and the little ones no longer had a home. And my kids, Linah and Amal, heard their mother saying something about them losing every-thing, including their clothes and toys. And so the little ones were asking if they can give some of their clothes and some of their toys.

So after the Israeli attacks and onslaughts, there is usually a lot of pain, a lot of trauma, and a lot of this, you know, poetic reaction. You want your kids to be generous. You want them to be selfless. But you don't want them to be talking about war in the context of war. You love your kids when they share their sweets or their clothes or their toys with other kids when they hang out. When this happens, it's so sweet, so beautiful. But at the same time, it's the kind of sweetness and beauty you don't want.

I usually like to talk about the siege being "tightened" in 2006, because there has always been a siege. When the occupation starts, when colonization starts, it besieges the people at the same time. It restricts the movement of people who want to travel, people who want to seek medical treatment, or who just want to travel for fun, for business, for studies.

I remember when I was in grade seven, and the teacher asked a question. There was a passage in the book that counts Arab countries, and there was a strange blank space in the middle, and he said, "Can anybody guess what's going on here?" We didn't know, we were little kids. He said the space was the word "Palestine" in Arabic. It was erased because the Israeli military controls the books that come to Gaza.

I remember an article from *Ha'aretz* from about five years ago, when an Israeli zoo was categorizing a gazelle as a "Palestinian gazelle," giving it the scientific name. And there was an uproar. Many Israelis protested, like, "Why are you using the word? You should be sued for this. You shouldn't say Palestinian at all."

This is the state of siege. Israel wants to control its people, and also wants to control us more, even the word "Palestine." I remember friends in the first intifada who spent six months in prison for raising the Palestinian flag or for having a tiny picture of [Palestine Liberation

Organization chairman] Yasser Arafat, or for sometimes wearing a T-shirt with a keffiyeh or something.

So the siege has always been that, what to wear, what to do, what to say, where to go, where not to go. But fifteen years ago, it was tightened to the extent of suffocation, when literally the Israelis were counting the calories entering Gaza.

It's a little bit better now, things improved a little bit. But it's improved because it's part of this political game. Gaza is being used as a lab. They test everything.

They want to starve us, to starve Palestinians. I think the unemployment rate reached 45 to 50 percent sometime in Gaza, too.

We've seen reports of Israel not allowing chocolates in. Why? Because they want to tell the world, to tell us, that we are going to control you no matter what you do. And this is what we refuse as Palestinians. We reject Israeli rule.

We don't want to submit to Israeli rule. And the more barbaric, the more brutal Israel goes, the more resilient and the more determined Palestinians become.

The leaders of today are the very little kids twenty years ago, seeing other people killed by Israel. And the Israeli terror, the Israeli massacres did not terrorize those people to become cowards, to give up, to say, "oh my God, we can't fight back, we can't." No. They grew up to be leaders. If you follow this from a military point of view, when Israel kills military leaders, the ones that come are more determined, more ferocious, in a sense, to fight back, to create new ways to hopefully contribute to ending Israeli occupation.

*

We have long given up on the international community, on America or Europe, because these are the very people protecting Israel and sending Israel the weapons.

In 2014, when Israel ran out of some kind of shells, I think, they just opened the doors to American warehouses inside occupied Palestine and they took as many as they wanted, because America is here to protect Israel. We see how Israel is even interfering in American politics, but no one wants to talk about that either.

So the Palestinian public opinion is that there is no way that officially America is going to do anything or Europe is going to interfere. All they can do is just lip service.

And the media is complicit, sadly. We've seen how even attempting to support Palestine—like, what happened with Ilhan Omar, for example, or Rashida Tlaib, how they are viciously attacked by American pundits on CNN and everywhere, accused of being antisemitic.

Palestinians have realized this long ago. And we are sad that the Palestinian official representatives still try to find a way among these supporters, to find help, and help is not going to come.

The only help that comes is the one that wants the Palestinian Authority to control us by proxy. Israel can no longer be inside Gaza or cannot be inside the West Bank 24/7, especially in areas where there is resistance growing every day. So: we give them money, we carry the weapons, you protect us.

So when it comes to the official media, this is how most people feel.

But we are very hopeful that the grassroots—the organizations, the unions, the people who vote—can say something. The more people take to the street, the more hope we have that this is going to have an impact.

One of the worst things about the media, the official media, is that I think sometimes they are more anti-Palestinian than Israel itself. Because there will always be accountability, this limited accountability inside the colony.

Israel says, "no, we didn't kill these kids." And now everybody says, "Israel didn't kill, Palestinians killed themselves." And then a couple of days later, they said, "oops, we did it." It was, you know, "we're going to investigate." But nobody else, not even on the personal level in the West, is going to be willing to say, "sorry, there is a correction."

Even in other massacres, we've seen how Israelis on social media, there are so many Israeli accounts and fake organizations, like Middle East Intelligence, run by Israelis who get, I think, money from Israel.

There was this guy who celebrated this, celebrated the attack, was saying Israel liquidated five Palestinian freedom fighters in Jabaliya. And then it turned out that this is actually a massacre. Five or six kids were killed, and then he deleted his tweet.

There was also a video, I'm not sure if you saw this, a video the Israeli army posted saying that we wanted to hit this house because there are missiles inside, but we didn't because there was a passerby. And a video cut to a soldier saying, "stop, abort." And then there was another Israeli official, a Twitter account, that posted the whole video.

And actually, like a moment after the video posted about the massacre was cut, there was another car coming to the place and the place was hit. So, in reality, Israel fakes this, fabricates many things. And many news media, in America especially, they copy-paste the Israeli press releases word for word.

What Israel says is usually the fact. What Palestinians say is usually doubtful: "according to Palestinian sources," "Palestinians say," "allegedly." But Israelis report facts.

This is very unprofessional. Hopefully, the change is going to come soon, but many people should be ashamed of doing this because it is not journalism.

*

Sometimes it's frustrating talking about this because it doesn't matter sometimes what we say. It doesn't matter what Palestinians say.

We keep shouting and screaming and, you know, reporting all over social media. Hundreds of Palestinians and pro-Palestinians, thousands of them, out there exposing Israel. And no matter how many of its crimes and massacres we've seen, Israel doesn't care. Israel kills with immunity. Israel knows it's not going to be held to account by anybody.

Israel is growing more ferocious. Israel is influencing American politics. AIPAC was bragging yesterday that 98 percent of the people they supported won the primaries. And this is incredible, spending over twenty million dollars, even supporting people who endorsed the attack against the Congress after the election when Trump lost, and people who refused to verify the elections that Biden won. People who are bad to America, because they are good to Israel.

*

In Gaza, when we talk about these [human rights organizations in the West Bank that Israel raided], it brings back what Israel was doing here when it was in Gaza. Universities, schools, organizations: all banned, all closed. The university where I studied, and where I teach now, was closed for years in the late eighties and early nineties.

For two, three years. It's just a university. Classes, teaching people English, Arabic, chemistry. Because Israel wants to control every tiny little aspect of our lives—whether this harms Israel or not, whether this exposes Israel or not.

Israel knows it's not going to be impacted by those [human rights] organizations documenting and reporting and exposing its war crimes and massacres. Never. They could impact, reach out to people who are on the fence, who don't know what Israel is doing. But Israel doesn't care about those people because they have, usually, Biden's ear or Trump's ear, influencing him.

So the attacks against these organizations must be put in the context that Israel has always been controlling us, controlling our lives. Because when you close these organizations, you also look at how many jobs you're going to lose when the people lose funds.

I know some of the branches these organizations have, they sometimes employ hundreds of people. It's the same when Israel attacks Gaza. Why would Israel bomb a high-rise building that has fifty small businesses that employ hundreds of people with thousands of family members?

So it comes in this context. Israel doesn't care about what these people, what these organizations do. We now have Israeli organizations which, again, Israel tries to ban—B'Tselem and others—despite the little work they do for us Palestinians. We don't think they're doing enough to bring Israeli leaders to account.

So when the very same thing the Palestinians are saying and documenting and exposing, is being documented and exposed by Israeli organizations, it means that, no matter how many Palestinian organizations Israel closes, the truth is going to come out. Because of the social media, because of the videos, because of the citizen journalists reporting 24-7. So why close these organizations?

Because Israel wants to be the boss. Israel wants to control our lives.

"It shall pass, I keep saying. Sometimes I mean it"

—2022

# They Even Keep Our Corpses: Dying in Israeli Prisons

*June 20, 2023*

Amid the backdrop of a usual family gathering in the late 1980s, where the laughter of my parents, uncles, grandparents, siblings, and cousins mingled with stories and teasing, my mind wandered off from the stories to match the kids to their parents. Yasser stood out, like an enigmatic figure, shrouded with mystery—always present, always favored, and always sad. Yasser had no father.

Exploiting a burst of laughter following one of my grandfather's quips, I leaned forward to my mother, curiosity getting the better of me. I whispered in her ear, "Who's Yasser's father?" Silence.

And as I asked the question, a bit of a lull took place, and the question came out as the shout of an oblivious eight-year-old child, piercing the air and disrupting the jovial atmosphere. The room fell into an uneasy silence, and the weight of the disapproving glares bore down upon me. At that moment, I realized I had stumbled upon a deeply sensitive subject.

Yasser was sixteen years old. His father, Oun Alareer, was tortured to death in an Israeli prison before Yasser was born.

With that haunting revelation comes Oun's story, one that is etched into the fabric of our collective memory to serve as a stark reminder of the enduring human spirit— unyielding in the face of adversity—and of the profound impact that one life, one absence, could have.

Since the Israeli occupation of East Jerusalem, the West Bank, and the Gaza Strip in 1967, about 237 Palestinian detainees have reportedly been murdered with torture, medical negligence, or execution during arrest or an attempt to escape prison.

Four Palestinian prisoners passed away in Israeli jails while on hunger strike, the last of whom is Khader Adnan, who died in administrative Israeli detention on May 2, 2023. Administrative detention is when Israel detains Palestinians indefinitely without trial or charge, usually for renewable six-month periods. Adnan is the first person— that we know of—to die from a hunger strike in Israeli detention since 1992. Months after his death, Israel still holds Adnan prisoner.

## *"Five minutes!"*

It was a cold February night in Gaza. Rafik, Oun's younger brother, had just put out the fire and gone to bed. The night was calm. The noises of the night creatures were some of the only things he could hear. The room was stuffy. Five siblings were crammed under their heavy blankets. The parents were in the next room. And Oun, who had been married only a few months, was in the adjacent room.

Rafik could not determine whether the hushed voices were due to the wind going through the holes in their walls. But his wonder did not last.

In seconds, the home's small yard was filled mostly with tall men with guns, the roofs occupied by snipers. They were Israeli soldiers.

According to Rafik, they separated the women, held them in a room, locked the door, and asked the men to stand against the walls, hands up. The women's weeping could still be heard despite the soldiers' aggressive shushes.

"Where's Oun?" came the question, coldly.

"Me."

Two soldiers pulled him aside and handcuffed him. Oun's father shouted, "Where are you taking him?"

"Don't worry. Five minutes, and he will be back," replied the short soldier.

*Seventeen days of torture*

But Oun never came back. This would be one of millions of Israeli promises that are not only broken, but turned into trauma and pain.

And just as they had less than a month earlier, Israeli troops came at night. This time, the household was silent in anticipation of any news about their son in Israeli prison.

This time, they could hear the troops tread heavily on the ground.

Oun had passed away.

The order of the Israeli military commander was that only the father, another family member, and the headman of the area (the mukhtar) could perform the burial rituals and lay Oun to rest. And it had to happen at night.

According to the headman's testimony, there was a massive gap in the back of Oun's skull, and his body showed a Y-shaped autopsy incision. The body told us that Oun's body parts may have been harvested. But what was certain was that Oun had been beaten to death.

Oun, as was later confirmed by his friends, refused to confess. He was tortured to death for this. His friends also later reported having their nails pulled out and their private parts electrocuted.

It is reported that Israeli authorities are still holding the bodies of thirteen Palestinians who were murdered in Israeli prisons. Israel insists Palestinians serve the remainder of their sentences, even if they are dead.

This vengeful practice deprives the bereaved families and relatives of bidding their loved ones proper goodbyes.

There is a 99.74 percent conviction rate in Israeli military courts of Palestinian detainees. Meanwhile, Israelis who attack or kill Palestinians almost never face justice.

Israel has imprisoned well over eight hundred thousand Palestinians since 1967. Currently, there are over 4,900 Palestinians in Israeli jails, of whom over 1,000 are under administrative detention.

## A *freedom fighter*

Oun Alareer was a freedom fighter. Born in Gaza in 1948, he witnessed the dispossession of his people, the lands lost, the refugees, the impoverishment of the natives, and then the occupation of Gaza in 1956 and again in 1967.

Oun was a member of a small, modestly armed group of fighters located east of Gaza City, namely in the Shujaiya neighborhood. The group carried out several successful anti-Israeli occupation attacks.

Some observers say that in the sixties and seventies, Gaza belonged to Israel during the day and to the freedom fighters during the night. It belonged to a handful of dreamers in their early twenties until Israel hunted them down. Some were assassinated or executed during arrest, and some spent decades in prison.

Israel outgunned them, determined to eradicate any Palestinian resistance.

And it was at night that heavily armed Israeli occupation forces broke into my grandfather's house and arrested my newly wed uncle Oun.

As a young man, Oun was often described as a very calm and thoughtful chap who was always there to help.

"He had brought two large tires to use as a weight to lift. He spent a lot of his time at the beach playing sports. He was tall and muscular. He loved basketball and football," his brother Rafik said.

"We never knew he was part of the resistance group in Gaza. He was very secretive. I often feared him like I feared my father, although he was only fifteen years my senior. He was a leader by nature. And Israel wanted to get rid of such people," Rafik continued.

*Déjà vu*

In 1991, Yasser, then twenty, applied for an Israeli permit (laissez-passer) to travel to Hungary for education.

"In my mind, I had to leave Gaza. My life was full of trauma. I was living in the shadow of a father I never knew. And Israel was killing Palestinian youths like me for nothing," Yasser says.

But his family, especially his grandparents, wanted him to stay. He is all they have of Oun. And the final word was for them.

"I was my father's age. Our courses were almost identical. I found a job. I got married. And my wife became pregnant.

It was like a déjà vu. Then the inevitable happened: I received a summons from the Israeli intelligence for interrogation. To me—and to everyone—we feared that mine and my father's tracks were identical."

The days leading to the date of the interrogation were intense. Fear and frustration intertwined, and its grip tightened as Yasser was allowed into the interrogation room.

It turned out the Israeli occupation authorities feared Yasser did not travel to Hungary because he was planning to avenge his father's death.

"Yasser, we know you are married. We know your wife is pregnant. If you ever think of wanting to become 'a hero' like your father, you will never see your child," barked the Israeli officer.

There was silence. Yasser could not talk back or defend himself.

And in a display of extreme cruelty, the officer's callous words echoed through the air, reverberating with the weight of a thousand fatherless nights. With a smirk, he brazenly boasted to the grief-stricken son, "I killed your father."

The room fell into an abyss of silence. Time stood still, shattered by the impact of those haunting syllables.

"It was like they killed my father twice."

For years and years, Yasser's world was made up of the walls of the cell where his father died. And although he learned to outgrow his pain and turn the stigma into an outlet the hard way, he is still very young at heart, yearning for a hug from his father that will never come.

"I want justice for my father. Is that much to ask?" Yasser insists.

Three youngsters in Yasser's extended family were named after his father. Oun is a name that always reverberates in our households in the hope of making up even a tiny bit of the pain his loss brought us. We will keep his memory always.

"Nusayba and I are a perfectly average Palestinian couple: Between us we have lost more than thirty relatives"

—2022

# Spyware Exposé Lets Israel Off the Hook

July 11, 2023

**Review of *Pegasus: How a Spy in Your Pocket Threatens the End of Privacy, Dignity, and Democracy* by Laurent Richard and Sandrine Rigaud, Henry Holt and Co. (2023)**

The TV host Rachel Maddow describes *Pegasus* and the story it tells as "freaking compelling stuff."

Maddow writes—in the book's introduction—that "it's an edge-of-your seat procedural about the heroes who found this dragon and then set out to slay it."

Authored by Laurent Richard and Sandrine Rigaud from the investigative journalism group Forbidden Stories, *Pegasus* is the outcome of a probe initiated by the leak of fifty thousand possible surveillance targets.

The investigation aimed to uncover the unlawful usage of Pegasus spyware against noncriminal figures, including human rights activists and journalists. Pegasus was developed by the Israeli company NSO—the initials of Niv, Shalev, and Omri, its founders' first names.

The book's authors do a fine job providing readers with an insider's perspective of the events during the investigation.

The Pegasus investigation team was led by Forbidden Stories and Amnesty International's Security Lab and involved a partnership with seventeen media organizations worldwide to reach out to journalists and gather evidence of Pegasus attacks.

The book documents the tremendous efforts by Amnesty's cybersecurity specialists, Claudio Guarnieri and Donncha Ó Cearbhaill, to design the security protocols that kept the investigation under wraps until publication and develop the forensic tool used to trace Pegasus in infected mobile phones.

*Pegasus* raises ethical worries around licensing the spyware to clients with poor human rights records and highlights the cases of journalists who have been abused by their governments, such as Omar Radi (from Morocco), Khadija Ismayilova (from Azerbaijan), and "the golden get"—as Dana Priest from *The Washington Post* described it—the case of Jamal Khashoggi and evidence implicating Pegasus in his murder.*

---

*Editor's note:* Jamal Khashoggi was a Saudi journalist killed by agents of the Saudi government on October 2, 2018.

The style of *Pegasus* is mostly anecdotal or exploratory, which allows for engaging storytelling. The personal connections to the story are emphasized.

Without doubt, the book can appeal to a broader audience beyond technology experts, given that the authors avoid technical jargon and explain complex concepts in a way that is easy to understand.

Pegasus is a tool for hacking and monitoring smartphones, compromising individuals, groups, and even entire governments. It can turn a device that we carry in our pockets or handbags every day into a spy.

The use of the spyware was initially reported in 2016. Over time, it has become more technically sophisticated with advanced features that enable it to infect phones without any action required from the target.

Rachel Maddow outlines in the book's introduction the enormous amount of information that Pegasus can steal: "That includes all text and voice communications to and from the phone, location data, photos and videos, notes, browsing history, even turning on the camera and the microphone of the device while the user has no idea it's happening."

*Vast sums*

Later in the book, its authors delve into NSO's history.

They note, for example, that NSO was set up in 2010. One of its founders Niv Karmi was at that time a "recently retired Israeli military officer, who specialized in intelligence."

In 2019, Benjamin Netanyahu—then (as now) Israel's prime minister—bragged that his government had invested "vast sums of money in military intelligence." These vast sums went to Israel's army—which has a specialist technology division known as Unit 8200—and to its spying agencies Mossad and the Shin Bet.

The book exposes how Israel uses Pegasus as a bargaining chip when developing relations with other governments. It is no coincidence, the book suggests, that Netanyahu's alliance with Viktor Orbán, Hungary's prime minister, became noticeably stronger "right around the time NSO licensed Pegasus to Hungarian authorities."

Laurent Richard highlights the role technology has played in Netanyahu's efforts to "create a united front against Iran in the Middle East." Richard explains that the Israeli government made sure to include "military-grade spyware" as part of Israel's "package of goodies" offered to tempt and seduce "prospective allies."

The Israeli government bore responsibility for approving licenses for the export of Pegasus. As the book states, Israel's defense ministry "had discretion to permit sales of the Pegasus system" so long as the identities of end users were kept secret.

Esther Hayut, the president of Israel's high court, has commented, "Our economy, as it happens, rests not a little on that export."

While researching the use of Pegasus, Richard interviewed Edward Snowden, who blew the whistle 10 years ago about a major surveillance program run by the National Security Agency in the US. Snowden lamented the lack of oversight mechanisms over Pegasus usage.

"There's no limitation," he said. "There's only Israel pinky promising that they're going to have their Ministry of Defense or whatever review the export license."

The Pegasus Project investigation team successfully identified more than a thousand people from an initial list. As well as human rights activists and journalists, they even included Emmanuel Macron, the French president.

While NSO's stated goal is "saving lives," it has contributed massively to the weaponization of cyber-surveillance by oppressive governments. The book demonstrates that NSO's denials that Pegasus was used to spy on Jamal Khashoggi and his loved ones were lies.

*Litmus test*

Despite acknowledging the role played by spyware exports in Israel's international relations, the book misses an opportunity to shed light on these relations' negative impacts on Palestinians and their rights.

A January 2022 article published in *The New York Times Magazine* by Ronen Bergman and Mark Mazzetti revealed how Israel used Pegasus to earn diplomatic gains. After being equipped with Pegasus, Mexico abstained from voting on several "pro-Palestinian" United Nations resolutions.

Bergman and Mazzetti noted that Panama supported Israel against Palestinians after installing NSO systems in 2012, while India shifted its position on Palestine after agreeing on the importation of intelligence equipment, including Pegasus. India opposed granting observer status to a Palestinian human rights organization at the UN's Economic and Social Council in 2019 despite India's past support for the Palestinian cause.

Front Line Defenders, a human rights organization based in Dublin, revealed in 2021 that Israel used Pegasus to spy on six Palestinian activists. That revelation is only briefly mentioned in the book's epilogue.

In total, the words "Palestinian" or "Palestinians" are mentioned only twice in the book and the boycott, divestment, sanctions (BDS) movement only once. The words "Palestine," "West Bank," and "Gaza" do not feature at all.

This is not just about words, of course.

The book ignores how Israel's weapons and surveillance technology have been "battle tested"—as makers of that technology say in their promotional brochures—on Palestinians. It is as if Palestinians do not exist or are not deemed to be worthy sources.

Similarly, *Pegasus* does not tackle Israel's history of spying on Palestinians. Unit 8200 is known to intercept private data about Palestinians—including information on their sex lives, medical issues and personal finances—so that the Israeli military can recruit collaborators through blackmail and extortion.

Palestine is a litmus test for journalists. Are they prepared to expose Israel's crimes against Palestinians, even if it means their own career prospects may suffer?

The authors of *Pegasus* fail that test.

*Randa Shehada contributed research.*

2023:

"A war against everything"

# Al-Aqsa Flood, Day 3

*October 9, 2023*

*Editor's note: On October 7, 2023, Hamas-led militants from Gaza attacked military as well as civilian targets in southern Israel. Hamas called the operation "Al-Aqsa Flood." Israel retaliated with a devastating ground and air assault that, by July 2024, had killed more than forty thousand people in Gaza and turned much of the territory into a howling wilderness. The Electronic Intifada podcast— comprising Ali Abunimah, Nora Barrows-Friedman, Jon Elmer, and Asa Winstanley—interviewed Refaat Alareer on several occasions as the horror unfolded. The transcript below has been edited for length and clarity.*

It's unspeakable brutalities. There's a bomb every couple of minutes. Whole buildings are being destroyed. Almost all the roads to al-Shifa Hospital were destroyed. So many families. No matter how many tweets you see, or how many livestreams you watch, the reality on the ground is a lot, a lot more terrible than it is on social media and on Twitter. *(Large bomb explosion)*

This whole room is filled with gunpowder, cement or [unclear]. My hair is filled with dust and cement, and the little kids behind me are terrified, in fear—the little ones. And we can see the pictures that follow quickly. Whole buildings, residential buildings, businesses, Palestinian infrastructure, schools, hospitals, ambulances, and medical centers. *(Large bomb explosion)*

You don't know whether this is, this is it. We don't deserve this. We're not animals like the Israelis think. Our kids deserve better. Israel knows that they want to punish the kids, the civilians. And I have always said this, even before, even from the nineties when young Palestinians praised those valiant fighters. They are to be praised. But if you know them in real life, when you see the pictures of those fighters, they're very simple people. They're lightly armed, modestly trained, but they have a weapon that Israel does not have: the weapon of the belief, the faith, that this is your land, that you are fighting a brutal European colonial enterprise that has been brutalizing Palestinians for over seven decades.

Those people—even from the nineties and later on, in the second intifada—they were always victorious when they came face-to-face with Israelis, always cost them losses in so many operations. And look at what happens. It's a miracle, actually, a hundred million miracles that took place. But it's all well planned, meticulously planned by people who have almost nothing except their faith. And those people believe that they're not only fighting for Palestine, they're fighting for the Ummah. They're fighting for a cause that is just, a cause that should not and cannot be forsaken. We believe that if we give up, then everybody is going to say: "Look at the Palestinians. They give up. Why don't you behave like the Palestinians? Why don't you bow down?" And Israel knows this.

Israel is punishing not, by the way, the Palestinian fighters. They are inside. They're inside occupied land. And many of those people from Shujaiya, from Jabaliya, from Khan Younis and Rafah, from everywhere, they have their parents and grandparents who have land behind the Armistice line. My grandmother used to point over there saying that when Palestine is free, you will be rich, because we have a lot of land that we can use to farm, to sell. But it's not ours because of the brutal Israeli occupation.

What I'm saying here, briefly, is that it's extremely horrible [what's happening to] the infrastructure. It's unprecedented. I'm not exaggerating, again, if I'm saying that this is the Blitz all over again, like what happened in London at the hands of the Nazis. Unfortunately, the Israeli Zionists who claim to be the descendants of the victims of the Holocaust are inflicting a similar plight, similar catastrophes against the Palestinians.

We know that it's very bleak. It's very dark. There's no way out. If there's no water, there is no way out of Gaza. What should we do? Drown? Commit mass suicide? Is this what Israel wants? We're not going to do that.

I was telling some friend the other day, that I'm an academic. Probably the toughest thing I have at home is an Expo marker. But if the Israelis invade, if they target us, charge at us, go door to door to massacre us, I'm going to use that marker, throw it at the Israeli soldiers, even if that is the last thing that I would be able to do. And this is the feeling of everybody. We are helpless. We have nothing to lose. *(Large bomb explosion)*

*

I just ventured out to the pharmacy to bring some medicine. My car was almost bombed five times. Just *(large bomb explosion)* driving for five minutes to the pharmacy to bring medicine to the little ones, painkillers and stuff. And you can only imagine how horrible it is. I took some videos *(large bomb explosion)* and these are—if you're counting, it's every couple of minutes. These are just the ones around where I live in the Gaza City, in Tel al-Hawa. And you can multiply this by a hundred times all across the Gaza Strip. It's not easy to call people. It's not easy to contact people, especially family members in Shujaiya most of whom had to leave their homes. Israel has just destroyed the Palestinian telecommunications company. We've no internet, no electricity.

I was just calling my daughter, and it took me like five tries just to get her to answer me. I am in touch with some of my friends, my students. I try, but I'm helpless. I'm teaching English poetry this term. I was teaching them your poem,

Ali. And they always love it. And I always tell them how poetry can be your weapon. It's your strongest weapon. But I'm lying to them. I think I'm lying to them if I'm telling them that this is your strongest weapon and Israel is pouring tons and tons of dynamite, of US-made missiles upon our heads.

I keep posting messages, trying to reassure them, sending prayers to my students and their families and loved ones, knowing pretty well that many of them will not be back and some of their family members, their homes . . . I'm getting messages just now that the Islamic University was targeted. I'm praying that this is not true. If that's true, that's like almost 1,500 people without jobs and 20,000 students without classes, without benches, without a university degree.

It's a war against everything. There is nothing that Israel did not hit. And there's just one message. It's a message of hate, of death, and destruction. That's it.

I don't like to say this, because I don't want to be using the Israeli captives as a way to dissuade the Israeli, so to speak, from bombing. But these bombs will definitely harm and hurt the Israeli civilians, so to speak, and soldiers captured in Gaza. But maybe Israel is bombing this hard so that they can kill those people, those Israelis, before they kill the Palestinians, so they don't have to free the Palestinian political prisoners.

We are dealing with people that are extremely horrible. Like, they are literally inciting genocide and taking words from the Nazi language and Nazi discourse. What else do you expect?

There was this, I think it was the Jewish Congress, that tweeted something about the Holocaust, that the number of Jews killed by the attacks from Gaza exceed the number of Jews killed on any one day during the Holocaust. And this is categorically, mathematically, statistically, it's wrong. And it's a minimization, trivialization of the Holocaust. But look to what extent they're willing to go. This is Holocaust denial, not only revisionism, because statistically it's not even close. But they are willing to exonerate Hitler and the Nazis in order to demonize the Palestinians and justify *(bomb explosion)* justify the upcoming genocide.

It's going to be ethnic cleansing. We don't know in a week if we're going to be in the sea, buried under the rubble or buried in graveyards, if there is space, or in Sinai pushed out to die in the desert.

*

*NORA BARROWS-FRIEDMAN: You've regularly talked about how you discuss this with your children. What are those conversations like now? It's evening, they're getting ready for bed. And we all hear what's going on outside.*

We're trying to huddle in the place, in the narrowest possible place that is less likely to be hit. That was like in the past. We don't talk a lot, sadly. In the past, I would spend time telling stories. But with the systematic attacks against

Refaat Alareer

sleeping Palestinians in their homes, and the extermination of more than twenty families so far—I read this number ten hours ago, maybe it's now double—we talk less. We eat less, we drink less. Everything is less. I try to hug [my children]. But it's very conflicting, very difficult. You don't want to hug them, so they don't feel that this could be the last one, and you want to hug them, so at least there is a hug out there.

And you want, you know, to pat on their heads. It's very difficult being a father here. Even expressions of intimacy and love are very difficult, because they could be interpreted in too many different ways. And the kids know. They feel all the lies we tell them, that it's going to be okay, that the bombing is far away. They're not working.

Now, even the first day, the first twenty-four hours, there were screams and shrieks all over the area every time there's a bomb. But now everybody is calm. This is the worst kind of trauma, the internal kind of fear and terror that the kids have to go through. I took a picture yesterday of my little Amal over here, opening her little notebook and reading her lessons.

Interestingly, Amal developed the habit of not liking school, not wanting to do her homework recently, but all of a sudden change happens. And she was reading stories for my wife. Nusayba tells me that she's an excellent reader. She's a second grader, but she reads well from books. Hopefully she grows despite Israeli death and destruction and genocide and becomes an amazing storyteller.

*

Since Saturday, we had around three or four hours of electricity. Some places where Israel hits very hard, they lose any access to electricity. And if there is no electricity, there's no water, because we have to use a water pump to bring the water. We have water every couple of days, sometimes more; sometimes once a week, twice a week. And then we fill the tanks. We fill the tanks, you know, until the next time. So no electricity means no water.

But where I live, we have a generator that could generate up to three to five hours every day. But we are using it as backup. Mainly now, the instruction from the management of the building is to conserve everything. Drink less, eat less, don't use water, don't take showers unless it's extremely necessary.

[I am] not sure if this is only a slow genocide Israel is doing. These are not empty threats. This is an Israeli prime minister, and they know this is going to cause uproar. But the international community is complicit. They no longer care, not even paying lip service to us. It's going to cause a tiny little embarrassment to Israel because, again, also using this threat and likening Palestinians to animals, to treat us like animals. It's what's going on on the ground . . .

It's worsening on all levels. Even the intensity of the bombings. They don't stop. In 2021, it would only mostly be the days, but now it's around the clock. In this talk, probably less than thirty minutes, we have had bombs around twenty or thirty times. And this is only in Gaza, in the city.

*

*ALI ABUNIMAH: Refaat, one of the things that Israel and its supporters always say is that they're not at war with the Palestinian people in Gaza. They're at war with Hamas, and the Palestinian people in Gaza are suffering because of Hamas and the resistance groups. And that one of their goals through these repeated massacres and bombing campaigns that we've seen now with accelerating frequency—2008, 2012, 2014, and then accelerating now multiple times a year—the goal is to, in their mind, to turn the Palestinian people against the resistance groups by making them suffer. So that people in Gaza will say to the Hamas leadership, "You did this to us, you brought these massacres upon us." From your perspective and from the perspective of people around you, is that Israeli strategy likely to work? Are people in Gaza going to blame the resistance for the horrifying situation that people are in?*

There are two points here. Hamas is thirty years old, I think. And this started well before Hamas, decades before Hamas. And not only in the years leading to the Nakba, the disaster, 1948. But even when the British Mandate enabled and empowered and opened the doors for the Jewish Zionists to immigrate to Palestine, empowered them, gave them weapons, weakened the Palestinians, destroyed the Palestinian resistance, so to speak.

So it's a lie. It's a fabrication that this is only because of Hamas. Hamas and other Palestinian factions and groups are a reaction to the Israeli occupation and brutality. The framing that Hamas is bringing harm is also insulting to Palestinians, because it negates decades of Israeli terror.

Look at the West Bank, look at the Palestinians in the 1948 areas. There is racism against them and apartheid. Look at the people in Jenin and Hebron and Nablus and al-Aqsa, al-Quds, Jerusalem. They're being brutalized every day. The settlements are expanding, and Hamas barely functions in the West Bank. So this is completely and utterly untrue. Israel is using Hamas to deflect the blame—that if Hamas stops, if Hamas is not in Gaza, we're not going to be to be doing this. And it's a lie.

The second thing is, Palestinians have learned a hard lesson that Israel is going to kill them no matter what. In 2014, when Israel wanted to eradicate Hamas, they killed people from the Islamic Jihad and from Fatah, and they killed 551 Palestinian kids, and like 200 women and 150 elderly people or so. So Israel does not differentiate. Israel kills all. The same thing happened again and again, in later Israeli attacks. And so many Palestinians realize that if Israel starts a war, it's going to kill anybody. Also, if you've seen the videos of people storming, it [was] started by Hamas. The whole attack was planned, executed, started by Hamas. But every Palestinian faction, even poorly armed factions with a couple of Kalashnikovs, participated in the attacks against the Israeli military posts. So framing this as because of Hamas is completely unacceptable. It's wrong.

The Palestinians find themselves cornered after being rejected. They tried every means of resistance. BDS? "Antisemitism." Great Return March? [Met with] violence, and snipers are sent. By the way, there was a report that the very snipers who killed and injured hundreds and thousands of Palestinians were either captured or killed in the [October 7] attacks. So the Palestinians find themselves in a corner where they can either submit, kneel—and even that is not going to be allowed in dignity.

You've seen the pictures, I think, of Israel capturing some of the Palestinians, and mostly they are not fighters, because they could have shown us the weapons. There were no weapons. Many Palestinian civilians entered there because they wanted to see Palestine, their villages and their towns, and those people were arrested, and they were humiliated. So even if Palestinians choose to submit, to surrender, Israel is going to humiliate them.

So for that, and for our belief in our right to defend ourselves, and the dignity of the free world, all Palestinians are in this together.

"Let's first survive together and then build together"

—2023

# Al-Aqsa Flood, Day 7

*October 13, 2023*

*Editor's note: This spoken interview with Refaat Alareer was conducted by Ali Abunimah, Nora Barrows-Friedman, and Asa Winstanley for the Electronic Intifada podcast. The transcript has been lightly edited for length and clarity.*

It's escalating, as you can see, the number of people killed, the number of children killed, the number of bombs Israel throws, the crazy procedures and steps Israel takes against Palestinians in Gaza. We always ask this question, what's next? And we can never predict. This is where you fail, whether you are a political analyst, a human rights activist, a veteran writer; you can't predict and you can't plan.

The topic of the hour is evacuating more than one million people from North Gaza. That's impossible. It's impossible to do for many reasons, because Israel still bombs people rushing out of this designated area.

There are two reports of two targets, people killed and injured; the roads are dangerous; the infrastructure is destroyed. So people are going to get killed anyway. And this is what many people realize. There are hundreds of thousands now in the Gaza City. And there are people who protested in the Shati beach refugee camp— Sheikh Radwan [neighborhood], I guess. They took to the streets, declaring that we're not leaving. How many times do we have to leave? How many people does Israel need to kill in order to be satisfied? How much blood? How many Palestinian kids?

But we're not also leaving because we don't want another Nakba, because next time Israel is going to push us into Khan Yunis and then into Rafah and then into the sea. And that's why some people decide to stay. Some people decide to go with their relatives and many people could be staying out in the street in this dangerous situation.

Every time Israel does this, throws pamphlets from the war planes that are as dangerous as the bombs, and then tells people to evacuate: a million people, half a million people, evacuate! And then people start saying, "I can't evacuate," or, "I don't want to evacuate." And then it's like: "Look, we are humane. We are good. We are cute. We're telling them to leave." And you can see this all over Twitter, for example, people saying "Israel told you." Even American politicians and journalists are saying, "but weren't you warned?"

So this is propaganda. This is a publicity stunt by Israel. And at the same time, it's dehumanizing, because Israel is going to say that, "Oh, Hamas is keeping them. Hamas is preventing them." Hamas is not preventing anybody. Hundreds of thousands left. And it's understandable, it's justified why they left. And hundreds of thousands did not leave, and it's also understandable and justified.

Those people are on their own. Palestinians don't have to wait for people to tell them what to do and what not to do. They are the most highly educated people in the area, among the top educated people. But again, it's always Iran. It's always Hamas. It's always this. It's always that. It never stops. Even when we ask for our freedom and human rights, it's usually not the Palestinians demanding this. Somebody else is insinuating them, is pushing them for a global agenda, an Iranian plan to control or to embarrass Israel.

And then comes this horror, unprecedented horror. No book, no words, no articles will be able to describe what we go through as Palestinians. It comes with a very systematic, nonstop targeting of homes or families and of people in their homes. Ninety percent of the people killed, 1,800 Palestinians, were killed in their own homes. And those people usually were hosting relatives and friends and neighbors, because this is what Israel said: "move." So people move. Where would you move? The schools are already full and also targeted. The UN, a couple of days ago, said sixteen people taking shelter were injured, and two of them were in critical condition.

So the schools are not safe. They're targeted. Most of the people killed in the Jabaliya massacre were people evacuating their homes from Beit Hanoun and Beit Lahia. It was a local market in the most densely crowded area in the world. And the number of people killed here is also reflected in the number of children. Somebody updated a couple of hours ago, and every time you refresh, you add twenty people or twenty children, two families, three families; we speak about more than fifty families exterminated. And I am also being very careful about the number; I think it's one hundred. The "Shehab family": it's the whole extended family, but they are actually five or six families. We speak about 583 Palestinian children in seven days. In 2014, Israel massacred the same number or fewer in fifty-one days. Now it is in seven days, and I did the math here.

We speak about four kids killed every hour, for seven straight days. This is extermination. This is annihilation. This is genocide. Yes. One Canadian TV said, "Well, isn't this a strong term?" I said this is what the Israelis are saying. They're saying, "we're wiping Gaza out." "But they're targeting Hamas," he said. I replied, "if you're targeting Hamas, you don't say we're going to turn Gaza into a city of tents." We're talking about hundreds of thousands of collateral damage. This barbarity is supported by America, Germany, Britain, France, Italy, and other Western countries sending money, sending billions, against a very small and very tiny space. Sending warships against Gaza! This is what's going on now.

*

*NORA BARROWS-FRIEDMAN: I'm struck by the media blackout here in the West about what it actually looks like and feels like for Palestinians right now, who are trying to move from place to place to place to find any semblance of safety for them and their family. Can you describe to us what it looks like when Israel carpet bombs the Gaza Strip, which is only about twenty-four or twenty-five miles long and maybe five miles wide at its widest?*

For us and [anyone] who is following the news, this is more than complicity. The other night I was with Chris Cuomo [of CNN]. He is in occupied Palestine and I was expected to speak for about twenty or twenty-five minutes about Israelis, poor Israelis, many of them admitting, "yeah, I am in the army. I was in the army. I'll join the army." And I was bombarded by all these, you know, humane stories of the occupiers, the settlers stealing my grandmother's land.

And then, unexpectedly—I've done dozens of talks and interviews, and each one of them starts with, "how's it going?" But the first question was about Hamas and not allowing people to [move]. And I was like, where do you get this from? Hamas would like for Palestinians with American passports to leave. But Israel is not allowing them to leave. It's not allowing anybody to leave. And then he keeps going on and even when he introduced me, he said, "Okay, wait a minute, you might be surprised." But he was too scared, really.

And at the end of the interview, I told him, Chris, your framing is riddled with inaccuracies, with fake news. And if you think this is what's going on, if you start the story from B, you blame the Warsaw Ghetto rebels, you blame the Native Americans, you blame the slaves that rebelled against the slave owners, and you blame the Palestinians. If you believe in this, then you're not paying attention. The political and media class, they're all in one club together, they care for each other, they benefit from each other. It's mutual. This class is now hellbent on demonizing and dehumanizing the Palestinians because they want to justify the genocide that is happening right now.

*ALI ABUNIMAH: People come to us for analysis. I don't know how to analyze this. I don't know what to say to people. Our hearts are in pain. Our hearts are broken when we see this world that allows the scenery that we're seeing in Gaza today. Massacre after massacre after massacre of whole families, of 583 children as of this morning—by the time we finish this livestream, the number will have gone up. And people digging in rubble in their bare hands. And this is a world that lectures us about human rights and democracy. I don't know what to say to you Refaat . . . I don't know how to face you and to face people in Gaza and I don't know how to say to you that I'm sorry we failed.*

Thank you, Ali. I think we didn't fail. When it all comes to the end: no, we didn't. We didn't submit to their barbarity. We didn't submit to their brutality. And even when this attack came, when Gaza was in its weakest time possible, look at what they did to the most invincible army in the area, the fourth strongest army in the world. The humiliation. But it's not only about that. This is not where we get our pride. We get our pride from staying principled at a time when everybody is not.

I saw a friend you know thrashing somebody who was posting some antisemitic stuff on Twitter. And he was like, "Don't do this! We're not them." And I was very proud. It is at this time that people, their metal can be tested: who they are and what their character is like. Those people failed miserably. We didn't. They failed because when it came to the Ukrainians—blond hair, blue eyes—everybody was sending money. Even the Israelis were posting pictures, how to make cocktail Molotovs. How little children are carrying guns and fighting the Russian barbarians.

Politicians competing to send billions of dollars to Ukraine, but when it came to people with darker skin, they failed and they failed miserably. And I don't want to say I don't know how they sleep because they don't have a conscience. There is this anti-Arab, anti-Palestinian, anti-Muslim sentiment that is deeply rooted and normalized in the media and among politicians. It's always been there, but it has just been exposed.

And I think there has to be a time of, you know, reconsideration. Muslims, Arabs, pro-Palestinians, free people all around the world: there has to be something that comes out of this, something stronger than before, more powerful, to learn the lesson that those people are unreliable, because some of those—even Bernie Sanders . . . I don't want to name names, but they were horrible.

People in the Congress, and everybody, saw this: Israel was heading towards a genocide. And you post ten tweets explaining why what happened from the Palestinians is wrong, for God's sakes. So, Ali, I think you didn't fail. We didn't fail as Palestinians. We stayed principled, believing that we don't want war. We want it to end because only poor innocent people get killed.

# Death 247 in Gaza

"Get up! Get up! You lazy ass!
We've got work, much work to do."

Nowhere in the world is death employed
So creatively like in Gaza
Death believes in diversity.
I whizz and bang and boom.
I fall with rain
Spread with air
And spring like water
Glow with the first light of the day
And do not go until I make sure
I have many a soul hitched to my tail.
I come for kids in tens and scores.
And when I finally rest
I beat my chest
Like this like this like this
And wish I won't go to work the coming day . . .

Death doth protest too much.
With kicks and clubs I wake
And go to work.

*October 14, 2023*

# In Gaza, We Have Grown Accustomed to War

*October 19, 2023*

Horrific experiences of death and destruction have permanently impacted Palestinians' culture, language, and collective memory. "Is it war again?" asks my little Amal, seven, memories of the previous Israeli assaults still fresh in her mind.

The wording of the question shows the maturity she has been forced to develop. Last year, Amal asked her mum if it was "another war."

Yes, it is war again in Gaza! In Gaza, we have grown accustomed to war. War has become a recurrent reality, a nightmare that won't go away. A brutal normality. War has become like an old grumpy relative, one that we can't stand but can't rid ourselves of either.

The children pay the heaviest price. A price of fear and nonstop trauma that is reflected in their behaviors and their reactions. It's estimated that over 90 per cent of Palestinian children in Gaza show signs of trauma. But also, specialists claim there is no postwar trauma in Gaza as the war is still ongoing.

My grandmother would tell me to put on a heavy sweater because it would rain. And it would rain! She, like all Palestinian elderly, had a unique sense, an understanding of the earth, wind, trees, and rain. The elderly knew when to pick olives for pickling or for oil. I was always envious of that.

Sorry, Grandma. We have instead become attuned to the vagaries of war. This heavy guest visits us uninvited, unwelcomed, and undesired, perches on our chests and breaths, and then claims the lives of many, in the hundreds and thousands.

A Palestinian in Gaza born in 2008 has witnessed seven wars: 2008–2009, 2012, 2014, 2021, 2022, 2023A, and 2023B. And as the habit goes in Gaza, people can be seven wars old, or four wars old. My little Amal, born in 2016, is now a B.A. in wars, having lived through four destructive campaigns. In Gaza, we often speak about wars in terms of academic degrees: a B.A. in wars, an M.A. in wars, and some might humorously refer to themselves as Ph.D. candidates in wars.

Our discourse has significantly changed and shifted. At night, when Israel particularly intensifies the bombardment, it's a "party": "The party has begun." "It will be a horrific party tonight." And then there is "The Bag," capital T and capital B. This is a bag that is hurriedly prepared to contain the cash, the IDs, the birth certificates, and college diplomas. The aim is to grab the kids and one item when there is a threat of evacuation.

The collective memories and culture of Palestinians in Gaza have been substantially impacted by these horrific experiences of war and death. Most Gazans have lost family members, relatives, or loved ones or have had their homes damaged or destroyed. It's estimated that these wars and the escalations between them have claimed the lives of over 9,000 (it was 7,500 when I started drafting this last week!) Palestinians and destroyed over sixty thousand housing units.

Death and war. War and Death. These two are persona non grata, yet we can't force them to leave. To let us be.

Palestinian poet Tamim Barghouti summarizes the relationship between death and the Palestinians that war brings (my translation):

It was not wise of you, Death, to draw near.

It was not wise to besiege us all these years.

It was not wise to dwell this close,

So close we've memorized your visage

Your eating habits

Your time of rest

Your mood swings

Your heart's desires

Even your frailties.

O, Death, beware!

Don't rest that you tallied us.

We are many.

And we are still here

[Seventy] years after the invasion

Our torches are still alight

Two centuries

After Jesus went to his third grade in our land

We have known you, Death, too well.

O, Death, our intent is clear:

We will beat you,

Even if they slay us, one and all.

Death, fear us,

For here we are, unafraid.

"It's very difficult being a father here"

—2023

# Israel Bombed My Home Without Warning

*October 22, 2023*

Israel bombed our building when we were inside our flats.

Our building consists of seven floors and twenty-one flats. Each flat hosts an average of seven people.

After Israel's latest major attack on Gaza began, some families evacuated the building for other parts of Gaza. Others took in relatives who had to leave their homes due to Israel's bombs.

I was among those who hosted evacuees. Four families—about twenty-three people—moved into our flat. All women and children.

The building we live in is considered a gem in the Tel al-Hawa neighborhood of Gaza City. We live in an area filled with about 150 buildings of five to nine floors.

We have a large power generator, fuel for a couple of months, and solar panels. That means we can generate electricity for our flats and for our neighbors and we can pump water for drinking and other purposes.

Since Israel's attack began, we have helped countless numbers of people to pump water, charge their electronic devices, and keep their freezers functional.

I believe that is a reason why our building was hit. We were helping people to live a "normal" life, despite Israel's attempts to starve us and eliminate the possibility of living with dignity.

Israel has now been conducting airstrikes on Gaza for a full two weeks.

Approximately 4,700 are known to have been killed. They include almost 2,000 children.

More than thirty thousand housing units have been completely destroyed.

Israel's latest attack can and should be described as an extermination of Palestinians in Gaza. It is genocidal.

*Propaganda tricks*

Our building was hit without any warning.

In the mainstream press and on social media, the Israeli occupation army is often "defended" as disciplined and even humane. That Israel gives prior warnings before bombing attacks every once in a while is often stated as a "fact."

The real fact is that Israel lies habitually. Israel's lies can easily be debunked if a little context is provided.

Yes, Israel does sometimes issue prior warnings. But such warnings tend to be at the beginning of its attacks. They usually come when a high-rise building is targeted and when the incident receives worldwide coverage.

The coverage supposedly shows that Israel does warn Palestinians before it targets them. And so, we hear such blanket comments as "but Israel warned them to leave" and "they are being used as human shields."

Again, these are lies.

By some estimates, Israel has not issued warnings more than 90 percent of the times it has attacked Palestinian homes.

That explains the huge numbers of people who have been killed. It explains how many families have been eliminated from the civil records.

Similarly, Israel's orders to "leave" are propaganda tricks.

When Palestinians leave their homes, many go to schools run by the United Nations. These schools have been targeted on many occasions, with the result that people who have evacuated their homes still get killed or injured.

Many more people stay with relatives and friends after evacuating their own homes. So, when a family home is bombed, the number of casualties is high and often includes evacuees.

In other words, when Israel pushes people out of their homes, it makes large numbers congregate in small spaces. So when Israel kills, it kills in tens and scores.

*Running for our lives*

Minutes before the explosions in our building, I stepped out of my flat and onto the stairs so that I could avail of my neighbor's internet connection.

I was making arrangements with a few contacts so that I could get the news out online about the genocide Israel is inflicting on Gaza.

The way we end chats has changed over the past two weeks. Before we would typically say inshallah—which roughly translates as "God willing." That has turned into, "if we survive."

Right before the strikes, I heard a rumble that was unusual. And without any warning: Boom!

It was so close.

Boom! I felt myself forced back against the wall.

The building shook. Smoke.

Gunpowder. Debris.

And Screams.

Men. Women. Children.

I rushed into my flat, the door of which was wide open due to the force. I shouted for everyone to leave.

"Get out!"

"Leave everything!"

"Take the kids! The kids!

Instinctively, the kids ran for their lives.

Some, though—like little Eman, six—were unable to move fast.

Eman had already been injured in a bombing last week. She has platinum in her left leg.

Eman's mother carried her and slipped. So my son Omar lifted up Eman and rushed out.

It took us a bit of time to carry our small bags of essentials—cash, gold, official documents, etc. Like all Gaza households, we had these bags at the door, ready to grab them in an emergency.

I had a last look, making sure that no one was still inside and then we rushed down the stairs.

Israel could have hit the building a third and a fourth time or it could have brought it down completely—like it has been doing with so many other buildings in recent days.

My family was lucky. Others in our building were not.

Um al-Abed and two of her daughters were in the kitchen preparing dinner for the family. That was where the missiles exploded, instantly killing Um al-Abed, tearing her body apart.

Her daughters—aged nineteen and seventeen—were also killed. One was buried under a lot of debris, the other was buried under the rubble.

A few other people were injured in the bombing and taken to hospital. But the first responders could not retrieve the bodies of Um al-Abed and her daughters, fearing that Israel would bomb them or bring the building down any minute.

Israel has even been attacking and sometimes killing first responders.

The impact of the missile blast damaged all the flats in our building.

Two were destroyed. Five flats, including mine, were severely damaged with cracks in the walls and ceilings. The others sustained substantial damage.

*Shelter in a school*

We do not know why the building was targeted. My mother-in-law insists it is because I talk to the media. Israel has now killed sixteen journalists over the past two weeks.

My mom also raised the same concern, "Do not write stuff online, my son. You know what I mean," she implored. She used the word "stuff" to avoid saying things clearly over the phone.

I told my family and relatives to gather in a particular spot and then to spread out. I got into my car and drove quickly so that I could help carry two children who had been injured from a previous Israeli bombing.

We met around the corner.

One girl—Lena—was missing. Her mother wanted to rush back to the building, still enveloped with smoke.

My wife held Lena's mother. And everybody started shouting, "Lena! Lena!"

What a relief it was when we heard my daughter Sarah say that she saw Lena with her grandmother.

For five minutes, we were lost. Confused. And exposed.

Some of us were barefoot, others with just one shoe.

We did not know where to go or who to call or what to do next. This was my first experience of being bombed and having to evacuate. I felt helpless.

And all of a sudden people rushed to help and check if we were ok. Some suggested we go to the UN school nearby.

We marched toward the school, dusty, bruised, tattered, and torn. The schoolyard was full.

People looked at us nonchalantly. It was as if they had seen hundreds of people join them after evacuating their homes.

But they made way for us as we joined a few more families in a small classroom.

"For my students, I'm helpless. I'm teaching English poetry this term, and they always love it. And I always tell them how poetry can be your weapon. It is your strongest weapon. It is what you need to do to carry on, to do this. I'm lying to them. I think I'm lying to them if I'm telling them that this is your strongest weapon and Israel is pouring tons and tons of dynamite, of US-made missiles upon our heads"

—2023

# The Five Stages of Coping with War in Gaza

*October 23, 2023*

Our familiarity with war in Gaza has led us to develop a unique perspective and unique coping mechanisms.

We can identify five major emotional stages that Gazans go through during these grim conflicts. The stages are denial, fear, silence, numbness, hope, despair, and submission.

This is day sixteen and Israel has killed over five thousand Palestinians (many are still unaccounted for under the rubble), including over two thousand Palestinian children, Gaza authorities tell us. Over fifteen thousand were injured and over twenty-five thousand Palestinian homes were destroyed. And Israel says it is ready for ground invasion.

*Stage one: Denial*

In the early stages of a crisis, there is often a sense of denial. We convince ourselves that this time won't lead to war.

People are tired of the recurring conflicts, and both sides may appear too preoccupied to engage in warfare. As missiles fall and soar, we maintain a form of partial denial, hoping that this time will not be as lengthy or devastating as past wars.

No, this time it's not going to be war. Everyone is tired of wars. Israel is too busy to go to war.

Palestinians are too exhausted and too battered to engage in a war. It could just last five days, give or take, we hope.

*Stage two: Fear*

Soon, denial turns to fear as the reality of another war sets in. Gaza is paralyzed as civilians, including children, are attacked by Israeli bombs. The pictures and videos of massacres, of homes obliterated with the families inside, of high-rise buildings toppled like dominoes turn the denial into utter terror.

Every strike, especially at night, means all the children wake up crying and weep. As parents, we fear for our kids and we fear we can't protect our loved ones.

*Stage three: Silence and numbness*

This is when Israel particularly intensifies the bombing of civilian homes. Stories are interrupted. Prayers are cut short. Meals are left uneaten. Showers are abandoned.

Therefore, amid the chaos and danger Israel brings, many in Gaza, especially children, withdraw into silence. They find solace in solitude as means of coping with the overwhelming emotion and uncertainty that surrounds them. Silence prevails.

Then numbness follows. As people attempt to protect themselves from the constant onslaught of distressing news, they grow indifferent. Because we could die anyway, no matter where we go. Emotional numbness sets in, as individuals attempt to detach from their emotions to survive.

*Stage four: Hope*

In the midst of despair, glimmers of hope may emerge. Even in the darkest moments, Gazans may hold onto the belief Israel might at least kill fewer people, bomb fewer places, and damage less. The most hopeful of us wish for a lasting ceasefire or an end to the siege or even the occupation. But this is merely hope. And hope is dangerous.

We hope that politicians will man up. We hitch our hope to the masses taking to the streets to reassure their politicians and warn they will be punished in future elections if they support Israeli aggression against Palestinians in Gaza.

*Stage five: Despair and submission*

Unfortunately, hope can often be fleeting, and many Gazans have experienced recurring cycles of despair. The repeated loss of life, homes, and security lead to deep feelings of helplessness.

In the final stage, there is a sense of submission as Gazans accept the reality that they are unable to change the situation. That they are left alone. That the world has abandoned us. That Israel can kill and destroy at large with impunity. This is a stage marked by endurance, as Palestinians strive to adapt and persevere in the face of ongoing challenges.

These stages of war have become an unfortunate part of life in Gaza, shaping the resilience and perseverance of the Palestinian people in the face of unimaginable hardships imposed by the Israeli occupation.

"I'm an academic. Probably the toughest thing I have at home is an Expo marker. But if the Israelis invade, if the paratroopers charge at us, going from door to door, to massacre us, I am going to use that marker to throw it at the Israeli soldiers, even if that is the last thing that I do"

—2023

# Al-Aqsa Flood, Day 20

*October 26, 2023*

*Editor's note: This spoken interview with Refaat Alareer was conducted by Ali Abunimah, Nora Barrows-Friedman, and Asa Winstanley for the Electronic Intifada podcast. The transcript has been edited for length and clarity.*

I want to start by quoting Wael Dahdouh.* Wael is a friend. I taught his son, Hamza, and I have known him for more than ten years. Amazing people, the whole family.

When he had to bid his son farewell, his family, and we realized later that one of his grandchildren was also killed in the deliberate attack. He said, these are tears of

_____

*Editor's note:* Wael Dahdouh is Al Jazeera's bureau chief in Gaza. His son Hamza was killed by an Israeli airstrike on January 7, 2024. Wael's wife Amna, son Mahmoud, daughter Sham, and grandchild Adam had earlier been killed by an Israeli strike on October 25, 2023.

humanity, not the tears of defeat or fear or cowardice. The Israeli occupation can go to hell.

And he used this beautiful Arabic word, *malesh*, meaning, it's okay, this shall pass.

And this is how we all feel, whether we were personally hurt, whether we lost our homes, loved ones, family members, extended family members.

We are experiencing unprecedented horror. Wherever you go. I moved to three places in the Gaza City, and not one is a tiny bit safer than the other. Not one of them. There is no place in Gaza, wherever you go, that is safe at all.

When our home was bombed, it was only a miracle, a godly miracle, that saved more than twenty-five civilians, mostly children; without a warning, without anything.

And of course, Israel and Israelis will always lie. "We warned them. We warned them to leave their homes. We sent warnings. We told them to go to the south." The majority of the massacres in the past ten days took place in the south.

So there is this feeling of fear, depending on who you ask. You know what the word I have been saying to my children, that I have been repeating to my children in the past week?

"Eat less, drink less." And every time I feel that this is going to be my last word, my last sentence to my children, to my kids.

I'm personally well off. Every day I bring home chocolate, candies, everything they want. Fruit, vegetables. But now nothing of this is there in the market, in the shops. The shelves are empty. And I keep telling them, "drink less, eat less." This is where we are here.

My older children can understand this. But how would you explain to seven-year-old Amal, who already survived three wars, and hopefully she will survive this fourth barbaric, genocidal war?

How would you convince her that the cookies I got should last us for two or three days? Because they were the last packs in the shop. How would you convince her that she should take only one piece, one cookie, rather than three or four or five, like she is used to in normal days?

But it's not only about food. This is not an aid issue. Palestine, Gaza is not an aid issue.

This is an extermination. Israel long ago created the concentration camp. But this is now an extermination camp.

We speak about more than 7,000 people killed in three weeks. And there are at least 1,000 or 1,500 people under the rubble. Just this morning, a few meters away, there were deafening, massive—we ran out of adjectives to describe how violent, how barbaric these strikes are.

And we were staying in a room with big windows to the street, and we had to go to the hallway to hide from the debris, because the debris keeps hitting the walls. And it went on for probably one hour. And guess what?

The first responders, the ambulances, couldn't arrive, couldn't reach the area until two hours late. And just now somebody was complaining, "why does the ambulance do this?" I said, because they have always been systematically targeted.

Before the extermination, there is this systematic way to push people into tiny spaces. I was just reading reports about a friend, somebody I knew some time ago, who was killed in 2021.

His wife was killed. His children were killed. His parents, his in-laws, his brother, his brother's wife, his brother's children. These are people I know.

They live in three or four different homes, houses, flats. But Israel bombed us into tiny corners, tiny spaces, so that they can drop one or two bombs and kill fifty people at one time, without having to throw even more bombs.

This is where we are now. Systematically targeting doctors. The other day there was a report of two doctors whose families were killed. This is punishment. What happened to Wael Dahdouh is punishment.

Wael is being punished because the Israeli liberal opposition leader, I forgot his name, said that if the media is reporting the facts, it's biased against Israel and with Hamas. If the media is presenting both ideas, both sides, it's also against Israel. It's very clear those people don't want the facts there.

That's why they're targeting civilians, targeting children, targeting families, targeting doctors, targeting journalists, and that's it. It's an extermination.

*NORA BARROWS-FRIEDMAN: We keep hearing of all of these bakeries and markets, one after the next, being targeted by Israeli missile strikes. How are people able to get food and water right now?*

It's too bad that we need to be talking about food and aid, but this is what Israel is turning this issue into.

In normal days, Gaza imports about five hundred trucks—imports, not Israeli aid, not anybody sending aid. We can import as many trucks as possible. With a siege that continued for more than twenty days, and then allowing twenty trucks and also trucks that would go only to the north and the middle area, and Gaza receiving nothing, no fuel for hospitals.

Three days ago, I documented my journey to the bakery nearby. I waited, queued for four hours and a half, and I bought bread for two to three dollars, probably one or two days. And in Gaza, when we speak about bread, this is what we eat.

Ninety percent of the food we eat in Gaza, we use bread to eat it. It's the staple. And yesterday, Israel bombed one of the bakeries nearby when they brought down a whole block in al-Jalaa Street.

There was no bakery yesterday. Today, I had to walk for about one hour and a half, went to three bakeries. The three of them were closed because they feel threatened and because they are running out of fuel, cooking gas, and flour.

And I just sent my son to see if any of the bakeries were open in the afternoon, and there were no bakeries and there was no bread. So we had no bread today.

*ALI ABUNIMAH: This has now been going for twenty days of total siege, cutting off food and water. Do you see the impact of that now on the population more broadly? What do you see in terms of the situation and people?*

First, usually there are, I think the rate was more than 60 percent of people under the poverty line in Gaza: farmers and laborers and blue-collar workers.

Those people usually work from one day to another. If they skip a day, if they don't work for a couple of days, they run out of money. So when the media asks me, I tell them, don't use me as a measure.

I have the money, but the shops are empty. I bought juice and stuff today, and I asked the shopkeeper, do you have anything in the stocks? He said, no more.

I said, how long are you going to be open? He said, around a week, and then we're going to run out of everything that can be eaten. People in Gaza are already slimming down.

In addition to the fear and horror on their faces, they are slimming down. They're losing weight, and it shows. Everybody is eating less.

People talk about how tired we are. I took a taxi on my way heading to a faraway bakery, and the taxi driver complained. He whined. He said, "It's too much. Enough."

One of the guys, an elderly man, probably the age of my father, he said, "We can't give up. They have already killed what they want to kill and destroyed what they want to destroy. We can't give up now."

We don't measure our lives by the days now. We don't. Even not by the hour. When I go out, I say, should I go left or right?

When I was waiting in the queue for the bread, the Israeli warships continuously for more than two hours were shelling from all over our heads. And a building, two buildings away, a flat was hit. And the guy in front of me received a call—

*(Connection cuts)*

"In Gaza, people can be seven wars old"

—2023

# What It's Like When Israel Bombs Your Building

*October 27, 2023*

I have six children. And so far we have survived seven major Israeli escalations, unscathed. We are an average family. My wife, Nusayba, is a housewife, I have two children in college and my youngest child, Amal, is seven. In Gaza, Amal is already four wars old.

We are an average family in Gaza, but we have had our fair share of Israeli death and destruction.

So far, since the early 1970s, I have lost twenty (and fifteen last week) of my extended family members due to Israeli aggression.

In 2014, Israel destroyed our family home of seven flats, killing my brother Mohammed.

In 2014, Israel killed about twenty of my wife's family including her brother, her sister, three of her sister's kids, her grandfather, and her cousin. And destroyed several of my in-laws' homes.

Combined, my wife and I have lost over fifty family members to Israeli war and terror.

*2023 war on Gaza*

As the bombs fall and Israel targets sleeping families in their homes, parents are torn between several issues.

Should we leave? But go where, when Israel targets evacuees on their way and targets the areas they evacuate to?

Should we stay with relatives? Or should our relatives stay with us, whose home is relatively "safe"? We can never be sure. It's been over seventy-five years of brutal occupation—and over six major Israeli military onslaughts in the past fifteen years—and we have so far failed to understand Israel's brutality and mentality of death and destruction.

And then there is the fear of what to do if—when—we are bombed. We try to evade them. But how can you evade the bombs when Israel throws three or four or five consecutive bombs at the same home.

The big question Palestinian households debate is whether we should sleep in the same room so when we die we die together, or whether we should sleep in different rooms so some of us may survive.

The answer is always that we need to sleep in the living room together. If we die, we die together. No one has to deal with the heartbreak.

*No food. No water. No electricity*

This 2023 war is different. Israel has intensified using hunger as a weapon. By completely besieging Gaza and cutting off the electricity and water supplies and not allowing aid or imports, Israel is not only putting Palestinians on a diet, but also starving them.

In my household, and we are a well-off family, my wife and I sat with the children and explained the situation to them, especially the little ones: "We need to ration. We need to eat and drink a quarter of what we usually consume. It's not that we do not have money, but food is running out and we barely have water."

And good luck explaining to your seven-year-old that she can't have her two morning eggs and instead she will be having a quarter of a bomb! (Israel later bombed the eggs.)

As a parent, I feel desperate and helpless. I can't provide the love and protection I am supposed to give my kids.

Instead of often telling my kids "I love you," I have been repeating for the past two weeks:

"Kids, eat less. Kids, drink less." And I imagine this being my last thing I say to them and it is devastating.

*Israel bombs our building*

If we had a little food last week, now we barely have any because Israel struck our home with two missiles while we were inside. And without a prior warning!

My wife Nusayba had already instructed the kids to run if a bombing nearby happened. We never expected ours to be hit. And that was a golden piece of advice.

I was hosting four families of relatives in my flat. Most of them were kids and women.

We ran and ran. We carried the little ones and grabbed the small bags with our cash and important documents that Gazans keep at the door every time Israel wages a war.

We escaped with a miracle, with only bruises and tiny scratches. We checked and found everyone was fine. And then we walked to a nearby UN school shelter, which was in an inhuman condition. We crammed into small class-rooms with other families.

With that, we lost our last sense of safety. We lost our water. We lost our food and the remaining eggs that Amal loves.

We are an average Palestinian family. But we have had our fair share of Israeli death and destruction. In Gaza, no one is safe. And no place is safe. Israel could kill all 2.3 million of us and the world would not bat an eye.

"Nothing kills like hunger"

—2023

# Israel's Claims of "Terrorist Activity" in a Children's Hospital Were Lies

*November 19, 2023*

On November 10, we woke up and found Israeli tanks right under our window. My family had been taking shelter at the Rantisi children's hospital for a few days.

What happened before and after we woke up that day demonstrates how Israel lies as a matter of routine.

Contrary to its claims, Israel deliberately causes destruction and damage. Its systematic attacks have been designed to make the functioning of Gaza's health system impossible.

We have been displaced since October 19.

That day, Israel bombed our building in the Tel al-Hawa neighborhood of Gaza City. Our apartment was left uninhabitable.

Following the attack, we took shelter at a nearby school.

We crammed with other families into a small classroom. There were two bathrooms for about two hundred people in our wing of the school.

We had left all our food at home. Some of the food was destroyed as our kitchen took a direct hit, destroying the fridge and much of our food reserves.

The situation at the school was, to say the least, inhumane and unsanitary.

Huge numbers of people were abandoned by the United Nations. Without any sense of shame, their vehicles promptly evacuated Gaza City and northern Gaza, when Israel ordered more than a million people to move southward.

*Hell unleashed on hospitals*

Having spent a few days at the school, I was offered the chance to shelter at a hospital.

It would have electricity and internet access. I wanted to be online so that I could report to the world Israel's extermination campaign against Palestinians in Gaza.

The Rantisi hospital was a lot better than the school. I thought that I would spend the whole time there until Israel stops its genocide.

That was before we got a notice. An Israeli flyer was circulated, alleging there were "terrorist Hamas activities" at the Rantisi hospital.

Many people shrugged off this threat at the beginning. Israel has been saying this kind of thing about Gaza's hospitals for a long time.

Then Israel unleashed its hell upon the hospitals and schools in the area.

Israel's troops surrounded the buildings. Israel bombed solar panels and the roof of Gaza's main psychiatric hospital.

Israel bombed the entrances to hospitals, causing deaths and injuries.

Israel had already bombed a local bakery and electricity poles and roads.

In other words, Israel is making life impossible in the northern half of Gaza.

People have no choice but to move southward—not that the south is in any way safe.

The next morning, more than two-thirds of the people sheltering at the hospitals had to evacuate.

Israel attacked people sheltering in hospitals, supposedly to send a message that there were Hamas activities inside them.

But no Hamas member could be seen and none were arrested as we were all forced to leave, with machine guns and tanks pointed at us.

Three days before Israel parked its tanks outside the Rantisi hospital, we were given cooked rice from the hospital's kitchen. It was to be our lunch for two consecutive days.

The rice was not cooked well and we already had lunch. So it was wasted food.

Nusayba, my wife, volunteered to make better rice.

I went with one of my in-laws to speak with the chef, preparing food in the Rantisi hospital basement. Hundreds of people were sheltering in that part of the hospital.

Hundreds of others were sheltering on the first floor. And the second floor. And the third.

The basement was open. There was not even a remote possibility that any captive could be kept there, not even for a matter of minutes.

The basement can be seen from the first floor on the northern side of the building. It has windows, so what happened inside was not a secret.

If cooking rice is a Hamas activity, then that was all that was going on in the basement.

*Terrifying*

On November 10, my daughter Shymaa woke me up and showed me a video of the Israeli tanks right below our window.

It was terrifying. The tank was huge.

I had never seen one so close.

Then we heard cries from all corners of the hospital.

We awakened the kids and prepared our bags.

We grabbed a few small bottles of water and some dates.

With Israel claiming there were Hamas activities inside the hospital, I did not expect anything good to come out of this situation.

It was necessary to speak. So I gathered about twenty-five people, mostly kids, together.

"Listen," I said. "I do not want anyone to cry and scream. I will be blunt."

I explained that there were three possible scenarios.

The first was that tanks were blocking the road to the west but that the road to the east was relatively open.

The second was that the Israelis might let women and children go and arrest the young men. I noted, however, that the Israelis had not brought buses for transporting people to any prison or camp.

"That leads me to the third scenario," I said. "They might let the women and children go and shoot the young men."

That point elicited a number of screams.

*Don't look back*

I continued by saying, "If that is the case, and I want to be clear, do not look back. No matter what happens to us. Do not scream or cry. Keep going east. Keep running."

Meanwhile, doctors at the hospital were frantically calling their bosses and the Palestine Red Crescent Society. The Red Crescent was not responding.

Two hours later, we received a WhatsApp message that the people in Nasser hospital—another hospital in the area— were preparing to leave. Hands up with white flags.

When they approached our gate, we rushed and joined them, carrying as little as possible, leaving behind most of our food and water reserves—just as we had to do when our home was bombed.

That Israel allowed everyone to leave is evidence that claims of "Hamas terrorist activities" at Rantisi hospital were lies. Not one of us was detained or even questioned.

We walked and we walked.

Many raised their hands and some raised a white flag. Everyone was carrying a bundle or bottles of water, even the little ones.

A few pushed their elderly parents in wheelchairs.

Some carried children.

Some carried family members who were injured.

One woman held a peacefully sleeping baby, barely three weeks old.

We headed east amid the rubble and debris. When I looked back, I saw two tanks with their barrels and machine guns pointed at us.

I had Nusayba, Linah, and Amal next to me. The rest of my children were nowhere to be seen.

We had to move—looking back could be perilous. I carried a huge bundle over my head and kept checking on Amal and Linah to make sure they were OK.

I asked them not to look back. They never did.

About twenty minutes later, we took a right turn and rested until the others showed up.

I left many of my belongings at the hospital. They included my clothes, a used laptop I had bought recently, a notebook, and a One Man Show bottle of perfume.

I heard that Israel found a notebook and a laptop and has been using them as evidence that Hamas kept Israeli captives in the basement of the hospital.

I don't know if the "evidence" belonged to me. But I want my stuff back!

There are still hundreds of thousands in the northern parts of Gaza Strip and the old parts of Gaza City.

We remain steadfast despite the bombs, hunger, and thirst, despite the genocide.

Every day we hear about Israel advancing and targeting water stations and solar panels and other equipment or infrastructure that are essential for sustaining life.

Almost everyone around me has a high temperature, a headache or an upset stomach. Many of Gaza's hospitals and clinics are now closed.

We fear that Israel could prolong the genocide.

What happens if the tanks remain in Gaza for another month?

Or two months? Or even more?

The mere thought of a prolonged genocide terrifies us because nothing kills like hunger.

# Drenched

On the shores of the Mediterranean,

I saw humanity drenched in salt,

Face down,

Dead,

Eyes gouged,

Hands up to the sky, praying,

Or trembling in fear.

I could not tell.

The sea, harsher than the heart of an Arab, Dances,

Soaked with blood.

Only the pebbles wept.

Only the pebbles.

"All the perfumes of Arabia will not"

grace the rot

Israel breeds.


*November 28, 2023*


*(An earlier version was published as "Doom"*
*on September 2, 2015)*

# On the Resilience of the Palestinian Community

*Transcribed from voice notes and published posthumously on December 11, 2023*

The Palestinian community, especially in Gaza, has always been strong. There is always this very strong sense of community, shared responsibilities, people caring for family members, even distant family members. This is part of our values, part of our customs and traditions—not only as Muslims, but also as Arabs, as Palestinians.

Even on the level of children and kids. I'm not sure if you hear them in the background, but I've never seen the kids in such harmony—playing together, sharing whatever dolls and games. They can fight, they can be naughty sometimes. But they've never been this harmonious. I've never seen this.

The sense of community, the sense of coming together, that we all can be killed at any moment—this sense is bringing us closer and closer. This is not to romanticize war. War is horrible. This sense of doom, the sense of death coming and the gunpowder and the non-stop bombardment. I'm talking to you and the tanks are probably three hundred or four hundred meters away from where we are in Gaza City. We could die anytime.

But we're clinging to our humanity, and this is what I keep saying. This could end up with the destruction of Gaza. Israelis promised to send Gaza back 150 years, to turn it into a city of tents. We could end up being displaced; a second Nakba, a more horrible Nakba than the first Nakba because this is being televised, streamed online, and on social media.

As Palestinians, no matter what comes of this, we haven't failed. We did our best. And we didn't lose our humanity.

I remember during the first days of the Israeli genocide, I went to a shop and bought powdered milk. Another person said, "Can I have one of these?" And the shopkeeper said, "Sorry, it's the last one." And we almost fought. I told him, "No, you take it." And he said, "There's no way I can." And I said, "I have one at home. Please take it." You must be familiar with how Arabs always fight at the cashier at restaurants, beating each other up to pay. It was beautiful—the man insisting he's not going to take it, and me insisting to give it to him. But he turned it down, declined politely, at the end.

When our building was bombed, we were at home. There was no prior warning and we had to flee, some of us barefoot. We just grabbed the bag—the famous bag in Gaza that families have near the door in every war with important documents, money, cash, women's gold, et cetera. So we ran away with nothing, no food. We left everything: the flour, the cooking gas, the eggs, the canned food, and we went with nothing to the school shelter and people were welcoming despite the fact that there were too many people. It was extremely difficult. We had very little water, very little food. The next morning, people who knew that we were bombed and came without anything to eat shared their stuff with us. That was beautiful.

Three days ago, there was a horrible bombing here. I went downstairs very quickly and there was a woman with two kids, and they were crying. I stopped and took two dates and gave it to the kids. The woman was surprised and the kids were silent; they were no longer crying. I believe it is contagious. Doing good is contagious. It makes you feel accomplished. It's rewarding in the way you help others. And it makes others help others. And this is what I want—for this to be infectious in the positive sense. And I see people doing this all the time.

"The Democratic Party and Biden are responsible for the Gaza genocide perpetrated by Israel"

—Refaat's last message, December 4, 2023

# I Teach English Poetry

*Transcribed from voice notes and published posthumously on December 11, 2023*

I teach English poetry this term and I have two hundred students. I posted an announcement on our Facebook group telling them I'm sorry that I can't help enough, I can't protect them as I should be as a teacher protecting his students. And I asked them to write—to write poetry, Arabic and English articles, and I did help some of them publish articles and pieces and poems as part of my role as a teacher, despite me being extremely under pressure, having my home and my building bombed, and having to evacuate to many places and shelters.

I usually summarize my policy as, to quote Hamlet, "I must be cruel to be kind." Tough love. I tell my students, "I'm tough because I love you, I care about you. I want you to be better students." So I worked them hard in terms of attendance and assignments and tasks and exams. Many students fear me generally in life. In university, even outside, they're usually cautious despite the fact that I try to be as friendly as possible. But again, a tough teacher is always feared, in a way.

I was queuing at the bakery and [one of my students] insisted on giving me his place and I insisted, "Never. Because Israel made everybody equal. He's killing everybody, he's starving everybody, making everybody suffer almost the same. I would never take your place."

I learnt from this student this beautiful gesture of offering me his place. Because offering me his place meant I could save an hour or more. And sometimes you could queue for two or three or four or five hours, by the way, and when you get close, they run out of bread. So that's a big sacrifice. Later on, I met [another] student of mine. I was queuing way ahead. He came, heading to the back of the line, and I met him and I insisted on giving him my place, as a reaction to that student offering his place. He was shocked and he said, "No, there's no way." I said, "I insist." Of course, he didn't take the place. He refused. But again, the gesture; the message was there. I'm sure he would do the same for others. You know, learn by example, by role models.

"We didn't fail. We didn't submit to their barbarity"

—2023

# Permissions

*Gaza Mourns Vittorio Arrigoni.* © 2011 Mondoweiss. Reprinted with permission from *Mondoweiss*.

*I Was Mustafa Tamimi.* © 2011 Palestinian Solidarity. Reprinted with permission from the website *Palestinian Solidarity*.

*And We Live On.* © 2012 Mondoweiss. Reprinted with permission from *Mondoweiss*.

*On a Drop of Rain.* © 2014 Just World Publishing. Published in 2014 by Just World Books.

*The Story of My Brother, Martyr Mohammed Alareer.* © 2014 Electronic Intifada. Reprinted with permission from *Electronic Intifada*.

*When Will Dad Come Back?* © 2015 Electronic Intifada. Reprinted with permission from *Electronic Intifada*.

*Israel's Killer Bureaucracy.* © 2016 Electronic Intifada. Reprinted with permission from *Electronic Intifada*.

*No Justice for Gaza Youth Killed in Viral Video.* © 2016 Electronic Intifada. Reprinted with permission from *Electronic Intifada*.

*Great March of Return.* © 2018 Electronic Intifada. Reprinted with permission from *Electronic Intifada*.

*Haunted by the Horrors of Cast Lead.* © 2018 Electronic Intifada. Reprinted with permission from *Electronic Intifada*.

*To Our Friend in Letters Dareen Tatour.* © 2018 Mondoweiss. Reprinted with permission from *Mondoweiss*.

*My Child Asks, "Can Israel Destroy Our Building If the Power Is Out?"* © 2021 The New York Times Company. All Rights Reserved. Used under license.

*Gaza Asks: When Shall This Pass.* © 2022 American Friends Service Committee. Published in 2022 by Haymarket Books.

*Raising Children Under Israel's Bombs.* © 2022 Electronic Intifada. Reprinted with permission from *Electronic Intifada*.

Refaat Alareer gained his Ph.D. with a dissertation on the poetry of John Donne. He taught English Literature at the Islamic University of Gaza, now destroyed. He is the editor of two collections of writing by his students, *Gaza Writes Back* and *Gaza Unsilenced* (both published by Just World Books). His journalism featured in *The New York Times,* and he appeared on the *BBC, ABC News,* and *Democracy Now.* He was a volunteer at the Gaza Zoo.